TRAVELS IN LADAK, TARTARY AND KASHMIR

9 788121 220071

TRAVELS IN LADAK, TARTARY AND KASHMIR

HENRY D'OYLEY TORRENS

GYAN

TRAVELS IN LADAK, TARTARY AND KASHMIR

HENRY D'OYLEY TORRENS

ISBN : 9788121220071

First Published 1862, reprint 2020 in India by

Gyan Publishing House
5 Ansari Road Darya Ganj
New Delhi- 110002 PH.011-43029145
books@gyanbooks.com

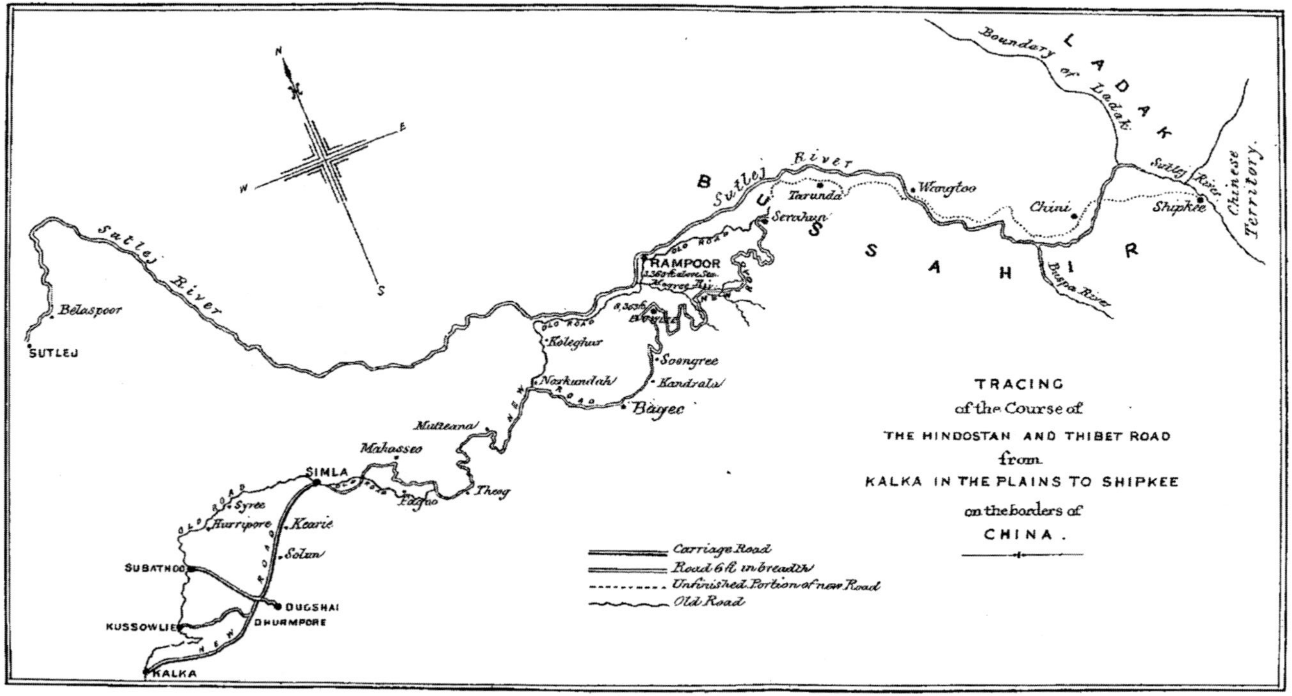
TRACING
of the Course of
THE HINDOSTAN AND THIBET ROAD
from
KALKA IN THE PLAINS TO SHIPKEE
on the borders of
CHINA.
Carriage Road
Road 6 ft. in breadth
Unfinished Portion of new Road
Old Road
N
E
W
S
LADAK
Boundary of Ladak
Chinese Territory
Sutlej River
BUSSAHIR
Shipkee
Chini
Buspa River
Wangtoo
Tarunda
Serahun
RAMPOOR
OLD ROAD
NEW ROAD
Koleghur
Soongree
Narkundah
Kandrala
Bagee
Mutteana
Mahasso
SIMLA
Theog
Fagoo
Syree
Hurripore
Kearie
Solun
SUBATHOO
DUGSHAI
DHURMPORE
KUSSOWLIE
KALKA
Belaspoor
SUTLEJ

PREFACE.

I FEEL that I owe the public some apology for venturing to intrude on their notice a book which must bear marks, evident to every reader, of hurried and careless composition.

Thus conscious of my audacity, I humbly confess that when I started on my travels I had formed no intention of ever recounting them; my notes and memoranda were therefore of the meagrest, although fortunately my sketch-book was pretty well filled.

A letter from my publishers, received some six weeks after my return, first suggested to me the idea that possibly an account of my wanderings might not be uninteresting even to the general reader. Upon this hint I commenced to write, and in three short months from the receipt of my publishers' letter, I had despatched to them the manuscript and illustrations of "Travels in Ladâk, Tartary, and Kashmir."

For enabling me to do this in the scanty moments of leisure which my duties allowed me, I have to thank, first, my memory; secondly, the diary of a fellow-traveller; and lastly, the able and interesting works of Bernier, Jacquemont, Moorcroft, Gerard, and Cunningham.

The proof sheets will be corrected by one of the companions of my journeyings, who will be in England in time to do so; and you, my readers, will have yawned or laughed over, been bored or amused, by the perusal of my narrative long before the publication will meet its author's eyes.

HENRY D. TORRENS.

Simla, in the Himalayas,
March 2nd, 1862.

ERRATA.

Page 99, last line, *for* "vidée," *read* "vider."
„ 100, line 1, *for* "un outre," *read* "une outre."
„ „ „ 2, *for* "ce petite cascade," *read* "cette petite cascade."
„ 107 „ 10, *for* "mœurs Thibétains," *read* "mœurs Thibétaines."
„ 179 „ 20, *for* "a la mitré," *read* "a la mitre."
„ 180 „ 4, *for* "il marmonne," *read* "il marmotte."
„ „ „ 5, *for* "resemblance," *read* "ressemblance."

SKETCH OF KASHMIR VALLEY FROM SOLEIMAN'S SEAT TO THE NISHAT BAGH

1. The Tukht-i-Sulymon or Soleiman's Seat
2. Here lies the Capital Sereenuggur and stretches away to the right behind the Fort. At this distance no houses are discernible
3. The Hurree Purvut Fort
4. The Nuseeb Bagh or Garden
5. Golden Island, or Sona Ki Lonkh
6. The Isle of Chunars or Chundee Ki Lankh (native name)
7. Shalimar Bagh
8. Nishat Bagh

CHAPTER I.

INTRODUCTORY.

I WILL commence by introducing to my readers the *dramatis personæ* who will, for the most part, figure in the foreground of the scenes I am about to picture to them.

We were six white men in all,—Lord

William Hay, Deputy Commissioner of Simla, and Superintendent of Hill States, who organized the expedition, and by virtue of his official position smoothed away many a difficulty from our path, and of whom, in the following pages, I shall speak as the "official friend;" Major the Hon. T. de V. Fiennes, 7th Hussars; Captain Clarke, 19th Light Dragoons, photographer to the party; two gallant young Riflemen, Lieutenant Buckley and Ensign the Hon. T. Scott; and myself.

Our intention was to march from Simla due north to Lè, the capital of Ladâk; thence westward to Sreenuggur, the capital of Kashmir; thence in a south-easterly direction *viâ* Chumba, and Kangra back to Simla,—in all, a circuit considerably over one thousand miles.

This scheme was carried out in its integrity by only two of the party, the others being obliged to leave us at different points along the route in order to join their regiments before the 15th of October, on which day expired their respective leaves of absence.

We went over no new ground: that is to say,

European energy had before explored every portion of our intended route; still it was known to but few—to an enterprising shikaree (*i.e.* sportsman) or two, a still rarer scientific traveller, or to the persevering members of the Indian Survey Department.

For travellers who, like us, were anxious to see as much as possible in three short months, and were not disinclined to rough it, I can conceive no better route, leading us as it did through every vicissitude of Himalayan scenery, over the high table-lands of Thibetan Tartary, into the verdant vale of Kashmir, and so back through the tamer but scarcely less beautiful scenery of the lower ranges of the Himalaya, to the tea-planted slopes of the Kangra valley, at which point the traveller may consider his wanderings in what has been called the Alpine Punjab at an end.

We were necessarily hurried, owing to our limited leaves of absence, and were therefore obliged to forego nearly all notion of sport. For on the Himalaya, and I believe all over the world, it is a recognised maxim, that in order to bag large game you must halt; but halt we could not, and many was the favourite haunt of ibex and wild sheep at no great distance from our route, which we were reluctantly obliged to leave unexplored.

A sportsman wishing to make the same tour as we did, ought in four, or still better, in six months, to make a capital bag without wandering very far from the actual track taken by us.

Our servants were mostly Hill-men, the exceptions being our *Chef de cuisine,* Ali Bux, and our "Khitmutgars," or table servants,—all swarthy Mussaulmen of the plains; also Mr. Terrear, or Terrear "sahib," as he was called by his fellow-domestics. A curious instance this of the influence of dress, mere dress; they knew Terrear to be a man of low birth—of a caste which they despised—their inferior, in fact, according to native ideas; he fetched and carried, had at times to suffer from the wrath of the Englishman, performed menial duties like themselves, and worked ten times as hard; but he wore his master's cast-off garments, and they called him "sir."

A Madrassee by birth, a Christian in creed, and colloquially a fair English scholar, Terrear was invaluable. He was an old campaigner, too, having been servant to an English officer in the Crimea, and therefore no stranger to the hardships of cold and wet, or the mysteries of life in tents. On this expedition he was Captain Clarke's factotum, valet-de-chambre, keeper of the privy purse, nay, cook too, on sundry and not infrequent occasions when his master's appetite could not brook the long intervals in our (in his opinion) slowly recurring meals; and last, not least, packer of chemicals, and photographic assistant in general.

I shall have occasion now and then to mention by name some of the other servants, so will here describe them. Bujjoo and Nurput rank first in the list, both vassals of the "official friend:" the former, bland and conciliatory, the latter, rude and energetic, represented in their respective persons a fair type of the two great principles, *suaviter in modo* and *fortiter in re*. These principles of action happily combined in the same man produce, we are told, executive perfection; and so it was with them; for actuated by the same wish, inspired by the same desire—the ensuring of their master's comfort,—this individuality of purpose made them, in fact, *one*, and produced results as perfect; for when Bujjoo's smooth entreaties failed to coerce refractory "coolies,"* or beat down extortionate "bunniahs,"† was there not Nurput there—Nurput of the heavy hand and unscrupulous tongue, to bully into submission? and again, when Nurput's violence had gone too far, and coolies showed symptoms of bolting, and bunniahs of sulkily shutting up shop, was there not Bujjoo there—Bujjoo the peacemaker, Bujjoo of the oily tongue, to restrain, to quiet, and cajole into good humour?

* Coolie, *i. e.*, labourer. Coolie is a term used all over India for common labourers, as distinguished from artisans, and with this exception, includes all those who by the sweat of their brow earn their bread. In this narrative coolies invariably mean carriers of loads—in fact, our baggage animals.

† Bunniahs, *i.e.*, sellers of grain. These men form a guild apart, and the food of the natives consisting almost entirely of grain, the Bunniah's shop is to be found in every village, and is the public place of resort, where the infidelity of Ram Buccus, or the levity of conduct of Dil Jhan, is freely canvassed.

Chumpa, the pitcher of tents; Noura, the king of the coolies; and my own head servant, Isree Singh, conclude, I think, the list of subordinate celebrities worth chronicling.

Our baggage was for the most part packed in "khiltas,"* and the whole of it carried on men's backs, so that we had daily to hire from the

KHILTA CARRIERS.

* "Khiltas" are cone-shaped baskets, covered either with leather or the undressed skins of sheep or goats, carried in the manner shown in the sketch. Those made expressly for Europeans are flat-bottomed, and have a wooden framework attached, which enables them to stand upright, and

villages on our route some fifty or sixty men to serve as beasts of burden for the day's march. A formidable number this for a but scantily populated country to supply, but thanks to the "official friend," and the exertions of the aforesaid Bujjoo and Nurput, we had seldom any difficulty in procuring them. Besides, anticipating delays of this nature, we had wisely provided ourselves with a reserve of coolies, in the shape of some thirty-five long-haired, sinewy-limbed, hardy Ladakhis, who marched with us the whole way, and to whose strong backs were confided our stores of provision, *batterie de cuisine,* &c. —a confidence which was never betrayed, for the *munitions de bouche* were always among the first arrivals in camp, however long the march.

These men formed the able-bodied portion of the inhabitants of a small village near Simla, occupied by emigrants from Ladâk, who had been induced to leave their native wilds by the (comparatively) high prices given for coolie

keeps them clear of the damp ground. The sticks shaped like a T, shown in the sketch, are used as a support to the khilta when the coolie is standing still.

labour in and about Simla. Their principal work consisted in bringing in from the forests in the interior, planks, heavy beams, and rough timber for building purposes. After loads such as these our burdens were light, and they walked away with our "khiltas," well filled though they were, as if they were knapsacks. Though not exactly suffering from the *maladie du pays*, nor indeed from any other malady, save perhaps hydrophobia, as far as regarded water for washing purposes, they yet seemed glad at the thought of revisiting *la patrie*, especially as they were well paid for going there.

Our tents were of the ridge-pole pattern, or, as they are called in India, *pauls*. They were six in number,—one served as mess tent, another housed the *élite* of the servants. Captain Clarke and myself had a tent a-piece, and our four companions doubled up in the two others. They were each of them, when dry, sufficiently light to be carried by one man, that is, the canvas part of them, the bamboo poles were tied in bundles, and formed two or three extra loads.

We carried with us a supply of iron tent-pegs,

a most necessary precaution, for wooden pegs soon split, and become useless after a little fair wear and tear; and in treeless countries such as Ladâk there are no means of replacing them.

A seventh tent there was, of dubious colour and uncertain shape, yet nathless a shrine of Art—nay, a very Temple of the Sun—devoted as it was to Terrear and photography: here, uncomfortably coiled up, crouched amid his chemicals, that unhappy pluralist was wont to sleep the sleep of the weary.

Having thus attempted to depict our expedition, both as regards its *physique* and its *matériel*, I will, with the reader's leave, postpone our start to the next chapter.

YE TEMPLE OF YE SUN.

CHAPTER II.

ON a rainy morning in the middle of July, the "official friend" and I turned our backs on Simla, and trotting briskly along the New Road,* reached Mahasseo in time for breakfast. We were in the saddle again at two, p.m., and leisurely proceeded on our way towards Mattianah, a distance of some five-and-twenty miles from Simla.

* *Vide* Appendix.

We thus knocked three marches into one; and purposing to do the same next day, counted on overtaking the Major of Hussars and the photographer, who, together with our servants, baggage, and other *impedimenta,* had started some days previously.

The rainy season was at its height; dense clouds of mist clung to the hill-sides, and clothed their summits with cowls of hodden grey, effectually concealing the beauties which on brighter days would have tempted us to linger on our road; and after some five hours' alternate riding and walking, we were not sorry to reach the Mattianah dâk bungalow, or post-house, as evening was closing in.

Here we halted for the night, and renewed our march towards Narkundah at daybreak.

Narkundah is justly celebrated for the magnificent view of the snowy range which the elevated ridge on which the dâk bungalow stands (nine thousand feet) commands; but on this tearful 18th day of July we were fated to see no such view. Thick curtains of cloudy vapour obscured the snow-white coverlid of the Alps which slumbered in the far distance. On our right, old Huttoo, a pine-clad giant some twelve thousand feet high, at intervals showed his gloomy crest, but not liking the look of the weather, turned in again sharp, like a sensible old sluggard as he was. It was evident they all voted the rain a bore, and had decided on being "not at home" to our anxious inquiries.

On leaving Narkundah we followed the New Road for some miles through a stately forest of lofty pine (the *Abies webbiana*, called "Pindrow" by the natives), of yew (*taxus baccata*), of oak (*ilex*), and holly (*quercus semicarpifolia*); then turning to our left, we commenced a pretty steep descent towards the valley of the Sutlej, over which, at a height of about four thousand feet, hangs the village of Kotghur, and about one thousand feet higher the hospitable dwelling of Mr. Berkeley.

This was our destination, and after about an hour and a half's rapid walking we found ourselves seated in his spacious verandah. Here, too, were our fellow-voyagers who had preceded us; the photographer already at work with his camera, despite clouds and fog. He had brought his lens to bear on the mountain we had just descended, and was patiently waiting for a ray of sunshine which *wouldn't* come.

Mr. Berkeley, or the model colonist, as the "official friend" called him, is a tea-planter, and the possessor of a considerable tract of country. He has been settled in the hills for some years, and is justly sanguine as to the results of his speculation. The Government has endowed him with limited magisterial powers, which he wields most judiciously, and is a living proof that the colonization of the lower hills of the Punjab by Europeans is not the mere chimera that many deem it.

His mansion—a long two-storied building—is a happy combination of the bungalow* of the plains, with the imitation of English comfort aimed at, but never reached, by hill architects. A wide and lofty verandah runs completely

* Bungalow,—Anglo-Indian for house, *unde derivatur*, I know not! but possibly so called from the sad bungles made by the Anglo-Indians of former days when they first dabbled in bricks and mortar.

round the lower story, and is repeated above on a smaller scale. This in the genial summer-time serves him as sitting-room by day and bed-room by night; and in winter, when he betakes himself to the cosy inner rooms, forms an additional barrier against the cold.

Next morning we sent on our servants and baggage to where, in the grey distance, our tents, already pitched, dotted the hill-side opposite—some five miles off only in appearance, but in very deed a weary twelve, for between us rolled, some thousand feet below, the rapid Sutlej; and here and there, with the aid of a field-glass, we could see the interminable windings of the tortuous path before us: but I anticipate.

It was a busy morning for the "official friend"—a shoal of intricate cases, beyond Mr. Berkeley's authority to settle, were awaiting the *burra sahib's** fiat.

The one which appeared to excite the greatest interest was a case of rent withheld; a cloud of dusky witnesses attended, but I must say, very

* *i. e.* Great Man, big-wig.

few obtained a hearing. The great man's decision, most promptly arrived at, seemed to satisfy all parties, and they went on their respective ways rejoicing. The said rent amounted to one shilling (eight annas) paid *triennially.**

The post which came in ere we left Mr. Berkeley's hospitable roof brought us a letter from Buckley and his brother rifleman. They had been delayed unavoidably, but would follow us by forced marches, and overtake us in no time. Deluded mortals! They little knew what was before them.

It was now high time for us to essay the rugged descent of which our field-glasses had given us a feeble notion, and after some five miles of stumbles varied by slips, and slips by stumbles, we reached the banks of the Sutlej.

Have you ever, on the Sussex downs say, or in any chalky country, gazed in muddy weather from the top of a coach on the road beneath till the brain grew dizzy with the rush, and the roar, and the whirling motion, till to your deceived vision it was the road and its sickly-coloured

* A fact.

mud that was gliding away from under you, not you over it? If you have, you can easily call up the impression produced on me as I stood on the narrow wooden bridge which spanned the flood, and gazed below.

It is of a hideous colour (caused by the washings-away of the white soil of Kunawur, through which it flows many miles above), and altogether a most unlovely river; but it inspires one with a strange sense of awe as its foul waters seethe below, fiercely cutting their resistless course the rocks between, for ever widening, for ever deepening their appointed way.*

* Sutlej. The most remote sources of the Sutlej are the eastern feeders of the holy lakes of Manasaravora, in N. latitude 30° 35′, and E. longitude 81° 35′, from whence it flows for about 280 miles through a country but little known, to its confluence with the Spiti river. The whole fall of the Sutlej to this point is 9400 feet, or 33·8 feet per mile. It then takes a W.S.W. direction for 180 miles to Belaspore: in this part the fall increases to 39 feet per mile. From Belaspore it takes a circuitous course of about 100 miles to Ropar, at the foot of the hills; from Ropar it flows past Loodiana in an easterly direction for 120 miles, where it receives the waters of the Beas river; thence in a south-westerly direction for 400 miles, when it receives the waters of the Chenab; to this point its length is there-

Born in the holy lakes of Manasaravora, he early leaps from their secluded lap, and roves a truant. From earliest infancy his steps are marked by a precocious wilfulness, and we must allow that from the cradle he experiences nought but the harshest treatment. He is soon joined by other wild young mountain water-sprites, untutored, uncared-for, and headstrong as himself; and to him they cleave, recognising a master-spirit, and become his devoted slaves, and in him lose their very being; and, behold! the headstrong child is become a turbulent youth,—swifter and swifter runs his race of life—louder and louder roars the din of his revelry; he laughs aloud in his new-found strength, crying for space—more space, and finds it—finds it in the Punjab's arid plain.

But this new phase of life is intolerable to

fore 1080 miles; after this the united stream is called the Punjnud, a name derived from its containing the accumulated waters of the Sutlej, Chenab, Beas, Jhelum, and Ravee.

The Sutlej is considered to be the Hesudros or Zaradros of the Greeks, and the Hypanis mentioned by Strabo.

It is the longest and the largest of all the Punjab rivers.

him, always shallow and superficial, with no great depth of character or channel, wedded for ever to the lean "ribbed" sand of India, who, warmest and most importunate of dames, holds him, despite his struggles, always, always, in her yellow arms: a sad change, this, from the fun of his tricksy childhood—the freedom of his gushing youth—the poor young man can't stand it any longer; bored to death, he resolves on suicide, and dies self-immolated in the waters of the Indus.

Readers of a geographical and matter-of-fact turn of mind, to whom this fancy sketch may appear unsatisfactory, will find a full, true, and particular account of the mighty Sutlej in the note, which has been compiled from sources the most reliable.

The bridge over the Sutlej at this point is a noble one of its kind, formed of lengthy *deodar** beams, supported at either end by piers formed of mighty timbers wedged for half their length in the solid rock; the other half stretches out over the gulf below, and is surmounted by other

* *Cedrus deodara.*

timbers, which overlap those on which they rest by some two or three feet; these in turn are

THE BRIDGE OVER THE SUTLEJ.

overlapped by others, and so gradually and cautiously the opposite buttresses yearn towards each other, and seem to strive to meet; then come the lengthy deodar beams aforementioned, and span the length between.

We had some misgivings as to whether our ponies would cross this somewhat perilous arch; for though the footing was of a good breadth, the low wooden parapet had on one side been stolen—for firewood, I presume; at any rate, *there* it was not, and the loose timbers creaked and trembled, and the entire structure heaved with our weight.

Our fears were, however, unfounded; the little animals walked over the slippery planks without jib, shy, or stumble; but smelling each successive board with a puzzled expression of countenance, walking "delicately" and with caution, and giving a heartfelt grunt of satisfaction on reaching *terra firma.*

Here and there the valley opened out, and showed a strip of flat cultivation along the river's bank, where the rice crop paraded its beautiful but fever-boding green, flourishing luxuriantly; and near a small village which we passed grew plantains and other shrubs native to the plains.

The contrast between the climate of the valley and that we had just left, was most striking; fever-impregnated and pestilential, with an atmosphere oppressively close, the short time we took in crossing it was long enough to give more than one of the party a headache. This, however, rapidly left us as the healthful breezes of the green hill-side, purer, cooler, and more bracing at every successive zig-zag of the precipitous ascent, fanned our cheeks.

What a road it was! Stairs? Well, they might have been stairs once upon a time,

THE ROAD TO MOSCOW.

planned by Titans when "children of a larger growth" had their being, and finished off and utterly done for by ages of snow-meltings, torrent-rushings, and that "constant dripping of water which," we are told, "doth wear away the hardest stone;" but it *was* a road! *A* road? It was *the* road—the *high road*, to—to—to Moscow! *Rien que ça!* And could we have foreseen and profited by another week's experience of hill-travelling, we should have called it "a fair mountain road!" But I try, reader, to give you my impressions of Himalayan travel as they first struck me.

We reached the summit without an accident, thanks mainly to the activity of our ponies. I congratulated myself during the ascent that none were there to see, for anything more derogatory to the dignity of a lord of the creation, more humiliating to one's *amour propre*, than to be dragged up a precipice pendant to the tail of a shaggy mountain pony, is difficult to conceive. For further particulars I refer the reader to the accompanying sketch.

We reached our tents about two hours before nightfall; they were pitched close to a large and tolerably well-built village, called Dilass. Our photographer, who, for artistic purposes, had preceded us by some hours, was there to receive us, and had caused, so he said, a fatted lamb to be killed for our evening meal. The flesh was lean, indisputably, and the flavour somewhat rank—suggestive of kid of goat (if kid it was), or rather of a patriarch of that hirsute flock. We were too hungry for severe criticism; but one and all arrived tacitly at the determination that not again should our artist order dinner. No!—*ne sutor ultra crepidam*—let him stick to his chemicals.

Serious doubts now began to suggest themselves as to the probability of our loitering friends—the riflemen—catching us up, and at a council of war held after dinner, we decided that, in their favour, a very short march should be made on the morrow. Instead of Kot, Tchuhai, some seven miles off, should be our resting-place.

After further deliberation, it was finally settled that a tent should be left standing for them, and that in it should be placed some cold viands and *one* bottle of beer! Reader, we had but two dozen! and so to bed, in that state of gratified self-contentment which the consciousness of having done something very good-natured never fails to create. Bujjoo, too, had announced that "chukor"* had been calling all round the camp ere our arrival; so anticipations of a good morning's sport mingled pleasantly with our dreams.

* The Francoline partridge.

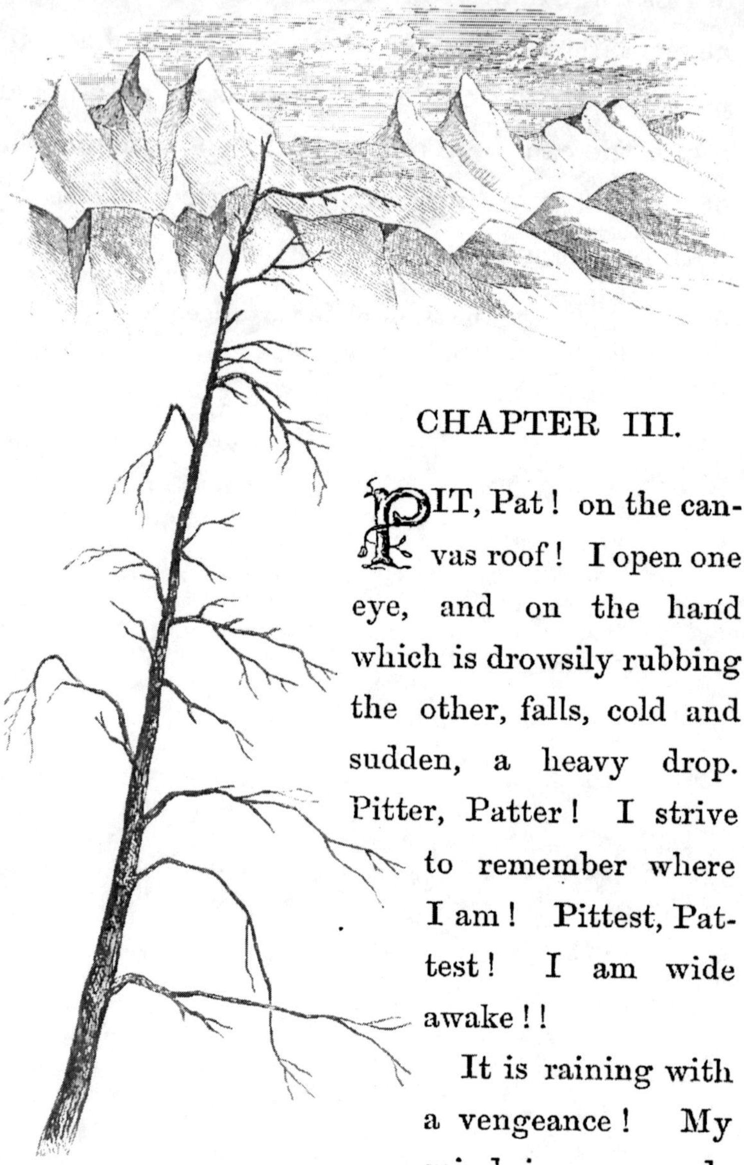

CHAPTER III.

PIT, Pat! on the canvas roof! I open one eye, and on the hand which is drowsily rubbing the other, falls, cold and sudden, a heavy drop. Pitter, Patter! I strive to remember where I am! Pittest, Pattest! I am wide awake!!

It is raining with a vengeance! My mind is soon made

up. Shooting on a morning like this is out of the question; and after taking precautions to prevent my being disturbed by any more cold drops which my "fair, false" covering of canvas might treacherously permit to filter through unchallenged, I, without an effort, relapse into sweet unconsciousness, return to the land of dreams (whence my absence has not been remarked), and there abide in peace till recalled to the damp realities of life by the entrance of the faithful Isree, who appeared followed by my "bheestie" (*i. e.* water-carrier), with water for my morning ablutions.

The "burra sahib" was up—had already been consulting with Ali Bux on the subject of breakfast — the other sahibs showed symptoms of wakefulness—in a word, it was time to get up! Such the substance of Isree's morning's salutation.

The rain had ceased, and we breakfasted in the open, while our servants struck the tents, packed the baggage, and dispatched them on coolie-back towards the next halting-ground.

We had the day before us, and but a short

march, so the ponies had a holiday, and we lounged lazily on, luxuriating in the bright sunshine, doubly grateful after so gloomy a morn. Now content with the beaten track which wound up the acclivity before us, now leaving it, lured by the defiant call of black partridge or chukor, which abounded wherever the hill-side afforded cover, or the narrow terraces of cultivation gave promise of a meal.

We shortly reached the summit of the hill overhanging Dilass, and turned to take a last look at Mr. Berkeley's house, now far away, but clearly visible—trim, neat, and whitewashed—the outpost of British civilization.

Our route now descended rapidly for a couple of miles, and then proceeded along the side of a well-cultivated valley, dotted thick with villages. One of these was the point fixed on as our halting ground, and towards it we hurried, for again was the sky overcast, and rain-clouds imminent.

Our tents were hardly pitched ere down came the storm, and from about four o'clock of this day, the 20th, to the morning of the 23rd, it rained with hardly an interval of sunshine worth the name. This we were, however, prepared for—it was only what we had a right to expect in the rainy season; and on the 21st and 22nd we trudged along wearily but hopefully through the wet, knowing that in a few marches we should be out of its influence.

Our halting-place on the 21st was Kot, a village beautifully situated on a rising ground, which would anywhere else be called a mountain, but compared with its surrounding alp, appeared to our rapidly enlarging intellects but a mole-hill—a conclusion to which we arrived *after* reaching its summit, *bien entendu.*

It *was* a lovely spot, for despite the miseries of wetted-throughedness, we yet took pleasure in remarking how above frowned pine-topped mountains, below stretched grassy glades, broken here and there into steep rocky declivities; and how around us the *cedrus deodora*, the cedar of the Himalaya, bent his lofty crest and waved his graceful arms as though in stately courtesy. *Stately* courtesy, did I say? Aye, so stately as to be quite chilling in its effects, for every wave of those graceful arms sent a shower-bath on the head of the unfortunate who trusted to them for shelter. It now blew a gale, and the tree-tops rocked before the blast, and we were not sorry to find an unoccupied habitation in the village, where we lit a mighty fire and essayed to dry our drenched habiliments. There we stood, steaming, dripping, round the crackling flames; there was no chimney, and the wood-smoke gracefully accomplished its exit through the open door, mingling with the purer, bluer, curling wave that rose from our cheroots, circling round and round, till an eddy from the leaky roof caught and turned it reeling out into the wet.

How good those cheroots were! Enter Terrear, wobegone and half drowned, but a twinkle in his eye shows that there's a deal of work in him yet. From under his coat he produces a black bottle! A momentary panic seizes us as the horrible suspicion suggests itself of some photographic acid drug!

"Would you honour like some whisky, sar?" A simultaneous shout of joy rings through the tumble-down shed, startling into animation the shivering Hindoos outside. They peer in, and perceive—*horribile dictu*—the "official friend" with his lips pressed lovingly on the mouth of the black bottle! There is no false modesty about that black bottle-ina; she sheds her favours on all alike, and "thrilled our very being." No, not "with the utterance of a name." Poor bottle-ina, bless her! is dumb, though she shows a proper spirit at all times. So we'll say, if you please—she

"thrilled our very being, with that sweet, long, mute caress."

Meanwhile, the coolies have been arriving one by one, slowly but surely toiling up the hill, and as the tents came up, dank and sodden with the constant wet, Chumpa, stripped to his shirt, which clings to his rounded limbs like an upper skin, seizes them, and rapidly spreads them out. "Puthar, burra, burra puthar," is his cry as he inserts one end of the stout bamboo pole into their languid folds. A heave, and up it rises; but Chumpa has over-calculated his powers. Heavy with wet, the canvas droops and threatens again to collapse, when Nurput to the rescue, and with a rush, and a shout, and some very bad language, that useful vagabond catches the tottering canopy! Two minutes more, and the close-packed mass of helpless canvas is a tent. A tent? A home for a king.

"Puthar, burra, burra puthar," cries Chumpa, and another tent rears its dripping form; but I crave pardon, reader! you, happy in your "blessed ignorance" of India, know not yet what "burra, burra puthar," means. I trust that "folly" will not be a necessary lien on the knowledge that friend Chumpa is an economical varlet, and hoards his tent-pegs as though they were golden ingots. A tent rope coiled round a weighty stone is as secure as if attached to a peg, however well malleted down; and to save his precious pegs, Chumpa used stones when he could get them. Now "burra, burra puthar," means "big, big stone" (subauditur, bring), and so our tents were pitched.

It grows late now, and in spite of whisky and cheroots, a still small voice from somewhere about the digestive organs makes itself heard, and "dinner! dinner!" is what it says.

It was just the very day for Indian servants to outdo themselves: surround them with luxuries, give them fireplaces, grates, ovens, and a park of *battéries de cuisine,* with meat the tenderest, and vegetables the most rare, and you will more than probably starve for want of a wholesome dish; but put them in camp in rainy weather, with no such appliances,—say you want dinner, and you will get a feast!

I do not mean to deny that the enjoyment of dinner depends greatly on the sense of anticipation; and that often when the chance of substantial fare is a very shadowy one—when you begin to think that you will have to dine off a cigar, and sup *à la belle étoile* — an unexpected meal, though intrinsically of villainous flavour, will delight your astonished palate,—simply because it comes *à l'improviste;* but allowing this, I will maintain that all Mahommedan cooks, especially Ali Bux, cook better under difficulties than in clover.

He had selected from our Ladakhis a scullion, the most ill-favoured menial that ever washed a plate. It was strange to see the two at work—to watch their antagonistic profiles bending over the flesh-pots; Ali Bux, with his close-shorn classic brow; and "Tom Sayers," so we called him, with brutish front and elfin locks:—the one tall, thin, stately, and aristocratic; the other dwarfish, thick-set, clumsy, and low-born; Ali Bux, whose

OUR CHEF AND HIS ASSISTANT.

finely-cut aquiline features harmonized well with his glossy moustache and flowing beard; Tom Sayers, whose plebeian want of nose equally well suited his thick, distorted lips, and coarse, unfruitful chin.

The *imberbis juvenis* hadn't a chance, in point of good looks, with his elderly Mentor; and I fancy it was in a great measure his sense of inferiority in this respect, which made him soon throw up the greasy appointments of scullion-general and deputy-turnspit, with the pay and perquisites thereto appertaining, and take to "khilta" carrying again. He soon got cheeky, *monitoribus asper; prodigus æris* he certainly was. It must have taken a lot of brass to beard that solemn follower of the Prophet; and, as to *cereus in vitium flecti,* he was like the rest of us. We are all just as bad as you, Tom Sayers.

The dinner bore out my expectations, and over its hot, savoury fragrance we vowed that Ali Bux was the Soyer of the East, forgot we had even been wet, and heard not the storm without.

It rained all night, and the morning broke more unpromisingly than ever.

Our road led us over the mighty shoulder of the Jilauri Mountain. At this it goes straight, without a swerve, without an apology for the extra exertion to which it is about to put you. No cunningly-devised zigzag is here to mask the difficulties of the way, and half-persuade you to lay the flattering unction to your soul that, after all, it is only a very gradual slope—long, perhaps, but very gradual. The stern reality stares you in the face without disguise; there is not the slightest attempt made to mitigate the incontrovertible fact, that up that infernal hill you must go, and what is more, you must go straight.

Rugged, steep, and stony in the best of weather, this uncompromising pathway naturally appears to the greatest advantage in rain like this; when down it pours a very respectable rivulet (respectable, I mean, in size—its habits are those of a most hardened vagrant), carrying with it all the loose *débris* it has strength to move, laying bare and bringing out into bold relief all the stern points of its channel's character, and adding to the natural amenities of the route a greasy slipperiness which, as you may imagine, tends greatly to aid the traveller's progress on his upward way.

But all things have an end, and there is a limit even to this interminable climb. A strangely-wild spot is the ridge on which you pantingly pause with a sense of labour o'er, of battle won; to the left stretches higher and still higher the continuation of the ridge on which you stand, blackly frowning through the thick clouds which wreathe Jilauri's front. Below you sweep weird masses of grey vapour fleeing before the conquering wind, that ever and anon, with a sudden blast, rends them to tatters; and peering through their scattered shreds, down beneath you, lo! it is bright sunshine, and green crops ripen, and flat-roofed hamlets nestle, snug in the genial warmth, unconscious of the mighty strife that rages so far above them. Once more the spirit of the mist rallies his scattered forces, and shoulder to shoulder, in serried rank, again they dare the headlong charge of the north wind's dread light cavalry; and the glimpse of peace below is hid from you, and in its stead suggests itself a sense of individual discomfort, for, fascinated by the grandeur of the storm, and exulting in that strangely-exhilarating sense of height, you have for the moment forgotten that you are but a miserable pale face, laying in a stock of future rheumatism and neuralgia. Now a shiver shuddering up from the soles of your laced-up boots to the crown of your drenched wideawake, recalls you to your own poor common-place insignificant self, and you toddle down the other side of Jilauri with but one idea predominant, and that is, a faint hope that you haven't caught cold!

The path down Jilauri towards the north-west, is, in comparison with its ascent from the south-east, quite a gentlemanlike means of communication, though strongly marked by the characteristic straightforward obstinacy of all the Kulu roads, which, as a rule, ignore the proverb, "The longest way round is the shortest way there;" eschewing all divergence, they make straight for their destination, and great indeed must be the obstacle that turns them aside.

The length of time which we took in reaching the bottom, showed almost more than the difficulties of the ascent, to what a height we had lately risen. (Jilauri is 11,300 feet above the level of the sea.)

We were now leaving the realm of wind and mist further behind at every step. It still rained, but with a noiseless, gentle downfall—not as above, with a spiteful, angry scud. At last, too, the longed-for sun appeared, and at his smile

Nature dried her tears, and laughed him back a welcome. A rude wooden bridge, which spanned a brawling brook, swollen with the late rains, offered us an almost dry seat on its moss-grown railing, and there we basked in the sunlight and abused Jilauri.'

It was no use going on; we had outstripped the coolies, and tents and baggage were all behind, so there we sat and watched the long line of "weight carriers" as they struggled down the mountain-side, with cautious step and slow.

But who is this coming along at a steady run, with bent back, but active feet? The coolies one and all make way for him as he rapidly passes them. As he draws near we perceive that he, too, has his burden—a small and light one, but carefully packed, and as carefully carried. He comes straight towards us, redoubling his pace, and makes obeisance; but his panting salaam is rudely interrupted by the "official friend," who, snatching the man's bundle, tears savagely at its wax-cloth covering. To our questions he makes no audible reply, but shies at our heads *pour toute réponse*, *Punches*, *Evening Mails*, *Saturday Reviews*, and, most welcome of all (with a mental reservation in regard to duns), letters from England!

It was the post!

Our halting ground, Jibeh, was about three miles on; the path followed the brawling brook aforesaid, and our tents were pitched ere the rain again came on. Our servants crowded under the shelter of a Deota, or small wooden temple of picturesque shape, which stood close to our

A "DEOTA."

tents; and altogether, the night of the 23rd was an improvement on that of the 21st. It still rained, but in a subdued manner, as if ashamed of itself.

The morning dawned without a cloud, and the tents were struck soon after.

At the next two halts, Platch and Largi, are houses for the accommodation of travellers. This is a great advantage, enabling one to send on the tents independently to Bujoura, a distance of about five-and-forty miles. Two deep and rapid unbridged rivers have to be crossed between Largi and Bujoura, rendering the absence of tents and all such *impedimenta* highly desirable.

The march to Platch is an easy one: the road continues to follow the brook, which increases rapidly in volume till, after about nine miles, it is joined by a good-sized mountain stream, which comes down from the high ground; on the right their united waters form a stream of some magnitude, which runs straight down the valley to Largi.

A well-built bridge of wood, of the same kind as that over the Sutlej, crosses the tributary from the right, and the road then follows the course of the stream to Largi. Platch is situated at the summit of a steep ascent to the right.

Here stands the house we had been told of—a small, square, two-roomed building, swarming with flies.

A funeral had crossed the road as we passed along. The body was swathed in white cloths, and carried on a rude bier of rough poles, in not the most reverential manner. The bearers went along merrily enough, nothing seemed to delay their rapid jog-trot, save here and there where a steep bit of ground made them go warily for their own sakes, or when the shoulders of one of them got tired, and he heaved his share of the load on to the shoulders of somebody else.

Three musicians led the procession, which did not consist of more than a dozen people. A fiddle of three strings, a drum, and "ear-piercing fife," were their instruments. The music was hardly of a solemn character. The performers appeared to be on the best of terms with each other, but their instruments were "at daggers drawn." The fiddle could never have *scraped* more than a *bowing* acquaintance with the fife, who on his part must have resented even that slight attempt at familiarity as an insult, for they were now decided cuts; and the drum, bored and distracted with their jarring notes, growled an "accompaniment" that was anything but agreeable.

There was only one mourner, and he a comely lad, with an earnest, melancholy look in his large brown eyes. The bearers ran carelessly down the slope towards the river, jolting their ghastly burden till the gaunt limbs were shaken from their cere-cloths, and shocked the eye with their stark, unnatural postures. Then the boy with the melancholy eyes seemed to remonstrate with them, but unseemly jokes were his answer, and the shrill scream of the fife drowned his appeals. Poor boy!

I watched the strange procession as it passed below, to where a strip of white sand stretched out into the meeting of the waters. Here was prepared a funeral-pile, from which soon arose a cloud of thick smoke.

We found on inquiry that the deceased was a zemindar, or landholder, in the neighbourhood. The boy, his youngest son; the bearers, elder brethren, friends, and kinsfolk.

At Platch we parted from our ponies, for whom the unbridged rivers in our front were obstacles insuperable. They started for a ford higher up, and would get, we were told, to Bujoura before us.

It is a weary walk to Largi—a weary sixteen miles along a narrow gorge shut in on either side by high rocky cliffs, whose base stood in the mountain stream which foamed along beneath us. I looked back shortly after starting, and on the small white strip of sand the zemindar's funeral-pile still smouldered. A solitary figure sat beside it. Poor boy! he must have passed an awesome vigil—black sky above, on this side and on that black waters rushing past, and his sole occupation the somewhat strange one of keeping papa alight. The sun beat fiercely down on our stony path, which reflected back his rays with a furnace-like heat and glare; but it was not as bad as the valley of the Sutlej, for now and then came a grateful breeze fresh from the snowy peaks which showed white in the far distance against the blue sky.

At Largi, a long low building, with a rude

verandah, guiltless of a door or window, was our shelter for the night.

We had a long day's work before us. Early to bed and early to rise was the order, and at five o'clock next morning we were at the river's bank, superintending the passage of the baggage by a "jhula," or rope bridge.

THE JHULA, OR ROPE BRIDGE.

The sketch gives a better idea of the reality of a rope bridge than 'any word-painting can. Every item of our property had to be slung over separately, in the manner depicted, and everything reached the opposite bank in safety. In fact, there is no danger so long as the ropes hold; you are tied firmly into your seat and remain passive and powerless during the operation. The sensation is not a pleasant one, especially when you are kept pendant in the middle to be photographed, as befell me; *barring* the sense of choking, and the wrench to your neck, it must be very like hanging. *My* Jack Ketch left me dangling in mid air for something like two minutes to give, forsooth, an air of interest to a photograph. I have sat for my portrait, but never sat I so still; remonstrance I knew was in vain, for the roar of the torrent beneath would have drowned the cries of a Boanerges.

My poor goats! they struggled vehemently for the first few seconds, but a glance below convinced them of the inutility of resistance. Realizing at once the horrors of their helpless position, they stoically resigned themselves to their fate.

It was tedious work watching the transit of other people's baggage, especially when there seemed to be no chance of an accident; so, having seen our own traps safely deposited on the right bank of the river, the Major and I strolled on up the path you see in the sketch, to where we hoped to find breakfast laid in some shady spot.

We had now, as it were, left the provinces, and were rapidly approaching the metropolis; before us spread the fertile valley of Sultanpore, the capital of Kulu. Our entrance into it shall be recorded in the next chapter.

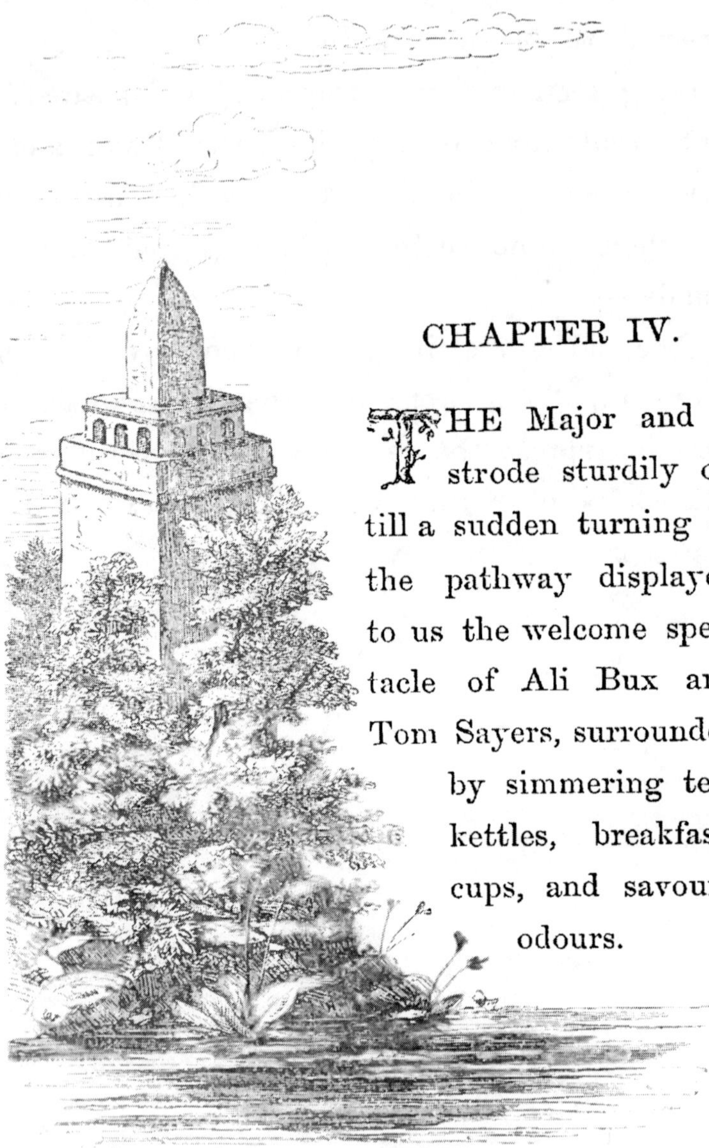

CHAPTER IV.

THE Major and I strode sturdily on till a sudden turning of the pathway displayed to us the welcome spectacle of Ali Bux and Tom Sayers, surrounded by simmering tea-kettles, breakfast-cups, and savoury odours.

Another minute, and we were reclining in a state of indescribable beatitude, tended on by willing slaves, who proffered first, a light for our cigars; next, a hot, fragrant cup of tea! It was, *barring* the ladies, a pagan's paradise. But here they come, tripping a-down the path before us, a laughing bevy of women and children, not houris, exactly, but country-folk of all ages! And here it strikes me that though we have been some six days in this fertile province of Kulu, not one word have I said anent its inhabitants. Let me commence by describing the merry party that is approaching us.

KULU WOMAN.

HEAD-DRESS OF KULU WOMEN.

Their features are good, generally, and of that type of which the children are pretty, the girls handsome, the mammas sternly featured, and the grandmammas positively hideous. Look at that group—child, girl, matron, hag; all are there, and yet perhaps not one of them has seen thirty summers.

There is one striking peculiarity about their dress: they "wear the breeches!" whether in

WOMAN OF KULU.

token of domestic supremacy, I know not, but it is possible that no such deep significance lurks in the costume, and that they are worn for purposes simply of warmth, comfort, and decency. However, I feel that it is out of place in pages professedly superficial to discuss a question so grave; we will therefore, if you please, leave it for the next scientific traveller to solve. Meanwhile, let me impress on you the fact—they one and all wear breeches!

And very nice ones they are—of silk frequently, and of a peg-toppy cut; above, very voluminous, but contracting from the knee downwards, till they fit tight over the slim ankle, and end just where a massive anklet of white metal confines the graceful limb, thus showing the whole of (generally) a very small foot.

So tight are they at the ankle, that how they ever get them on is a puzzle. The Major suggested that perhaps when once on they never take them off; but I trust, reader, that you will, with me, scout such an idea as an unwarrantable and malicious suspicion.

A chemisette with short sleeves, and reaching below the waist, covers the upper part of their persons; but it is in the head-dress that most scope for a display of taste is given: their hair, plaited into one long tress, is wound round the head in turban-like folds, and looped up over a little black flat hat of woollen cloth with a turned-up rim (a pork-pie hat, in fact), which is worn either demurely straight, or coquettishly on one side, according to the caprice of the wearers; and to give a certain piquancy to the charms of this little hat, a little tassel is added. Picture to yourself a bright-eyed, well-featured, nut-brown face peeping from under this "coiffure," and agree with me that the effect is charming.

The nut-brown complexion is a good lasting colour, that the sun does not freckle by day nor the frosts chap by night, but it is not proof against the crows'-feet of Father Time—wrinkles, alas! begin to show themselves ere girlhood is past!

I regret to say that they are apt to feign a luxuriance of hair which does not exist; but they do it in so ingenuous a manner that you forgive them; the skeins of brown worsted with which they lengthen their dark tresses are so unmistakeably brown worsted, that out of sheer pity for the transparency of the attempt at imposture you forgive it. In fact, I own to some slight compunction of conscience in thus betraying these frailties to their European sisters. But let me make amends by declaring it to be my firm opinion that they do it with no wish to deceive; that it is as much a custom with them to wear brown worsted ends to the glossy tresses, as it is to wear silk continuations of masculine cut.

I also regret to say that nose-rings and *goîtres* are both very prevalent.

Moorcroft says that "the common garb of the poorer classes is little else than a blanket, which is first wrapped round the waist; one end is brought over the shoulders, and fastened across the breast with skewers, and the other is passed round the thighs, and secured to the waist; the legs and feet are bare." Some of our coolies answered this description exactly, but it is but right that I should add that they were all of the male sex.

The well-to-do men wear little flat hats like the women, woollen peg-top trousers, and a sort of woollen smock-frock, fastened round the waist with a girdle—a most sensible and comfortable costume; in cold weather, a blanket worn as a plaid does duty as a great-coat.

But on seeing us the laughter of the merry group has ceased, and they try to pass as if they didn't know we were looking at them; it is only the children—bless their honest eyes!—who honour us with a good stare. Our knicker-bockers, however, are too great a novelty to be passed quite unnoticed, and I catch one young lady, with sidelong glance, taking mentally a pattern of my nether garments, with a view, doubtless, to an interview with her milliner on her return home.

Now "coolies" begin to pass us in rapid succession, and soon up come the "Official Friend" and the photographer, Terrear bringing up the rear, acting for the nonce as baggage guard, and whipping up the stragglers.

Their arrival is the signal for breakfast: it is soon despatched, and Ali Bux is ordered to hurry on, for we have many miles to go and another river to cross before nightfall.

The scene before us was a most lovely one: we looked straight up a green valley some two or three miles broad, which stretched away till the eye could no longer distinguish where its fertile slopes ended, or where the mountains which bounded it began; above these again rose peaks so unearthly in their purity, that but that they moved not, we should have called them clouds.

Glittering down the centre of the valley rolled towards us the Beas river,—now broad, still, and placid as a lake—now confined in a narrower channel, racing on with rush and roar till it entered a deep gorge on our left; here it seemed so to curtail its fair proportions that it was difficult to persuade oneself that this narrow, dark, smooth stream was the same as that which just now seemed to fill the valley with its broad bosom.

"Still waters run deep;" such the solution of the puzzle.

In about another mile or two it fell in with the stream we had just crossed, and turning suddenly to the right, swept on towards the plains.

Author, loq. (who has evidently been studying the *Friend of India*).—" What a glorious valley

Where could Government find a better place to try the experiment on a grand scale of European military colonization?"

Official Friend.—"Where, indeed? but 'first,' as Mrs. Glass says, 'catch your hare.' The land is not Government's to give. Look around you! All available land is already under cultivation—every inch of it belongs to native proprietors, who, as you perceive, make very good use of it. There is not room for the European."

Author.—"Where is the difficulty? Purchase the land, offering ample compensation to the native."

Official Friend.—"But the land is not for sale; and it would be an act of arbitrary tyranny, only to be excelled by actual ejectment, were Government to insist upon the sale of this people's paternal acres. No! if Government wants to colonize, the only thing to be done is to purchase from the native proprietors whatever land there may be in the market, and to retain for disposal to settlers, as required, all '*lawaris.*'"

Author (completely puzzled).—"What the deuce do!—pardon me—I would say, what is the meaning of the term '*lawaris?*'"

Official Friend (with a benign smile, and in an instructive tone).—" 'Lawaris' means land going by default of heirs, to which Government has as yet rarely, if ever, asserted its right, being content to make over such estates to any one with the shadow of a title to them, or, in default of a claimant, to the first person who might offer to guarantee the Government assessment."

"But," continued the Official Friend, "the only land, as far as my experience goes, thus available, is forest land, uncleared, and at a high elevation; the fact of its being uncleared is in itself a formidable obstacle to the settler, and the fact of its high elevation a still more difficult one to surmount, for it is above the possibility of irrigation.

"Now want of water is the principal difficulty which native cultivators in the Himalayas have to fight against—there is a great deficiency of water at above a certain, and that a very low, elevation."

Author.—"The cultivation of tea does not require much water; potatoes, too."

Official Friend.—"Granted; but the cultivation of tea requires capital, which your European military settlers have not got; and as for potatoes, natives will always be able to undersell a European who attempts to grow them with a view to making a livelihood thereby. I can't see myself how a retired soldier, settled on a piece of land which he may do what he likes with, can make a livelihood; but grant that it is possible, will he do so? A retired soldier, freed from the restraint and discipline of a regiment, is not likely to work very hard. Military life in India tends no doubt to the formation of idle habits, and a pensioner is a man jealous of control, not well disposed towards the natives, and not unfrequently addicted to the bottle."

Author (who does not like to hear his cloth abused by a civilian who cannot possibly know anything about it).—"Oh, pardon me! I can name instances—look at So-and-so, &c.—all respectable members of society, hard-working and well-conducted!"

Official Friend.—"I do not deny it. But the men you speak of are not agricultural colonists, living far away from the rest of their countrymen; they are artisans carrying on thriving trades in European stations, and themselves employing a great deal of native labour. They are, besides, exceptional cases. *I* speak of your average soldier, and I am right in my estimate of him.

"In fact, I think myself that Government would commit a very serious political error if it goes out of its way to induce European soldiers to settle as agriculturists; the chances of success appear to me so slight, the attendant difficulties so great, that though Government is bound to afford every assistance to the man who has made up his mind to seek a fortune as a settler, it should be, at the same time, exceedingly cautious not to encourage hopes which are so unlikely to be realized.

"Then the settler must marry! Whom? Whom but a native woman? Not one in ten can hope to take to wife an English woman. Not a very pleasant prospect for the philanthropist to contemplate, especially when he gives a thought to the character of the consequent progeny.

"What greater curse can befall a country than

to be overrun by a race of half-breeds—endowed with all the bad, deficient in all the good qualities of the parent stock?

"Again, suppose the settler married to a white woman! What a fatal country is this for the children of European parents. We have been now one hundred years in the country, yet there is not one recorded instance of a third generation—the descendants of Europeans."*

Author (shifting his ground).—"But in Java?"

Official Friend.—"Java! Oh, I am ready to admit that the system of culture obtaining in Java would alter the case very much, for by it Government can compel the native landholders to devote a certain portion of their holding to the cultivation of sugar, tobacco, tea, &c. This system has doubtless its advantages, and would unquestionably create a larger demand for common European labour; but then Government must be prepared to do what it does in Java—to bind itself to purchase a certain portion of the

* *Vide* Dr. Chivers on "Means of Preserving Health of Europeans in India."—*Indian Annals of Medical Science*, January, 1859, page 380.

produce at a certain rate, to make large advances without interest to European and native speculators for the purchase of machinery, &c. &c., without which the said produce would be of no value. But such interference with the native landholders is opposed to our practice, and repugnant to English ideas generally."

Author (beaten at all points).—"Then you are of opinion that it is only by the cultivation of exportable products—such as tea, &c. &c., which requires a considerable outlay of capital to commence with, that European colonists can thrive in the hills?"

Official Friend.—"*Himalayas,* mind! not Neilgherries."

Author.—"In the Himalayas; and as military colonists have no capital, European military colonization is a myth! eh?"

Official Friend (slowly and sententiously).—"Q.E.D. But we must make a start; it's time to be moving."

After a walk of some miles we ascended to the bank of the Beas, where another novelty in river transit awaited us.

About thirty natives, stripped to the skin, each provided with a *deri*, or inflated buffalo

DERIS IN THE WATER; MANNER OF PADDLING.

hide, were busily paddling our servants and baggage across the stream, here of great breadth, and running with a current so rapid as to carry the paddlers some distance down ere they reached the opposite bank; then, shouldering their hides,

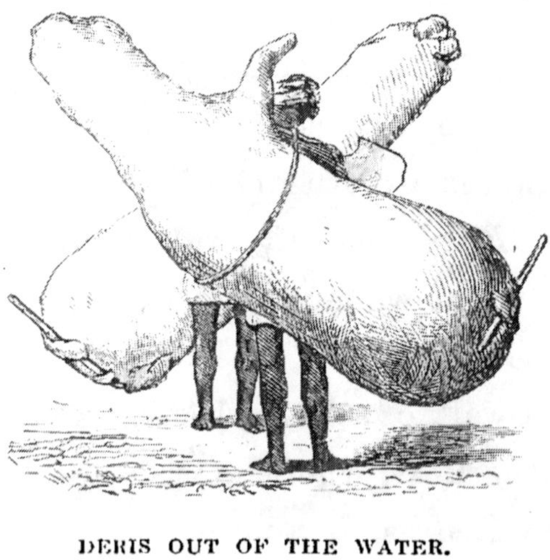

DERIS OUT OF THE WATER.

they marched up the side to a point a good way above, and entering the water again, paddled back for a fresh load.

Such quaint, odd, shapeless things! and yet not without a semblance of the live buffalo they once kept warm. Once in the water they lose all originality of expression, and are so evidently in their element, and at their ease, that you trust yourself to their buoyant backs without hesitation. But watch them emerging dripping from

DERIS OUT OF THE WATER.

the stream! See the feebly pompous, and helplessly inflated air with which they mount their owners' backs! Centaurs reversed, pawing the air with nerveless stumps of legs, and solemnly nodding and bowing to each other as the ferry-men stop to chat, and you can hardly persuade yourself that they are not alive!

I have never seen anything to compare with them in monstrous absurdity—save perhaps the strange specimens of the insect world that the microscope discovers in every drop of water.

Poor beasts! It is sad to reflect that however perfect their health may have been when alive, their hides are doomed inevitably to constantly recurring and frightfully severe attacks of flatulency!

Moorcroft gives so good an account of them that I will quote him.

"The skins used for this purpose are those of bullocks, which are stripped off in this manner. An incision is made in the back part of a hind leg, almost the whole length; and the skin being flayed off from the hock upwards is turned forwards, the same management being observed as in the process technically termed casing a hare, except that the skin is cut through below and round the knees and hocks, the legs being left adhering to the body. The hide is then doubled up and buried for a few days, in order to suffer so much decomposition as will favour the separation of the hair, which is rubbed off by the hand, or a blunt wooden knife, without abrasion of the skin. The skin is then turned inside out, and the natural openings of the eyes, &c., stitched up: it is then turned back again, and the main incision sewed up with thongs of raw hide. The open ends of the limbs are tied, except one, which is left open as a tube by which to inflate the skin. The thin tar procured from the deodar and other species of pine, is then poured into the skin, and shaken about in it until the flesh inside is well charged with it, and it is then tanned exteriorly by steeping it in an infusion of pomegranate husks. When required for use the waterman blows into it through the hind tube, and ties up the opening. A double thin cord is fastened round the inflated skin, across which the waterman places himself on his chest, holding the string with his left hand, whilst with his right he manages a short oar, assisting his passage with his hands and feet. Sometimes a piece of stick is tied in one of the legs, and left projecting from it for the waterman to hold instead of the string. The passenger, with as much baggage as he can carry, sits astride the ferryman's back, with his knees bent, and resting on the skin. When heavy and bulky articles are to be transported, two skins are brought together, the ferryman of each laying hold of one of the projecting legs of the other skin, and a frame or raft supporting the burden, lies across the backs of both: a charpai, or Hindoostanee bedstead, forms the most convenient raft. Horses and mules are led over, the waterman holding them by a string in one hand, whilst he paddles himself and his human load across in the manner above described. When not inflated, the skin is slung over the back, and carried about without any inconvenience. No expedient seems equally well adapted for the transport of large bodies of men and baggage over the most rapid rivers, or so likely to be serviceable as a wreck-buoy or float, to be carried on board ship. The cost of a 'deri' is usually a rupee and a half (three shillings), and its weight not above sixteen pounds. A couple of deri-men usually accompany persons of rank hunting in the hills, in order to carry them across the mountain-streams, the rapidity and fury, if not the depth of which, render it impossible to ford them without such assistance."

The Major and myself stripped and bathed a little higher up. We told each other that it was very jolly, and that we enjoyed it immensely; but our shivering limbs and chattering teeth gave the lie direct to our protestations. It was snow-water, not long emancipated from its parent glacier!—I shudder as I write!

A few miles more and we reached our tents, pitched close to Bujoura, a small village commanded by a fort now in ruins; but it must formerly have been a place of some consequence. Moorcroft, who saw it some forty years before, calls it "a large square fort belonging to Kulu. It consists of square towers connected by a low curtain, the whole built of hewn stone, strengthened with beams of fir." And no doubt in those days, before our occupation of the country, afforded a great protection to the Ladâk merchants from robbers and other illegitimate leviers of black mail, and at the same time checked smuggling and enforced the payment of the then Government's tolls.

Chumpa met us with a broad grin on his honest face; but to our inquiries about the ponies he could give no satisfactory answer—they hadn't come; that was all he could tell us.

Not far from our encamping ground some enterprising speculator had commenced a tea-plantation: a melancholy Baboo, whose tent was pitched hard by, superintended its cultivation. His desponding air seemed to have affected the plants, which drooped their heads in sickly guise, a sad contrast to Mr. Berkeley's healthy shrubs.

That night, fatigued by the long day's work, the "Official Friend" and our artist retired to their tents betimes, leaving their two companions meditatively smoking the pipe of eve.

"Do you know," said the Author, "those were monstrous sensible remarks of Hay's about colonization; and though, of course, it's utterly ridiculous for a civilian to——halloo! where are you going?"

The Major (sidling towards the tent door)—"Oh, monstrous sensible remarks!—ar—ar—good night!—mons'ous sensible." (Exit precipitately.)

Author (solus)—"Well, it is devilish odd that whenever a fellow wishes to have a little rational conversation——" (Exit grumbling to bed.)

I trust, reader, that our conversation of this morning did not bore you as much as it evidently had done the Major.

"FEEBLY POMPOUS, AND HOPELESSLY INFLATED."

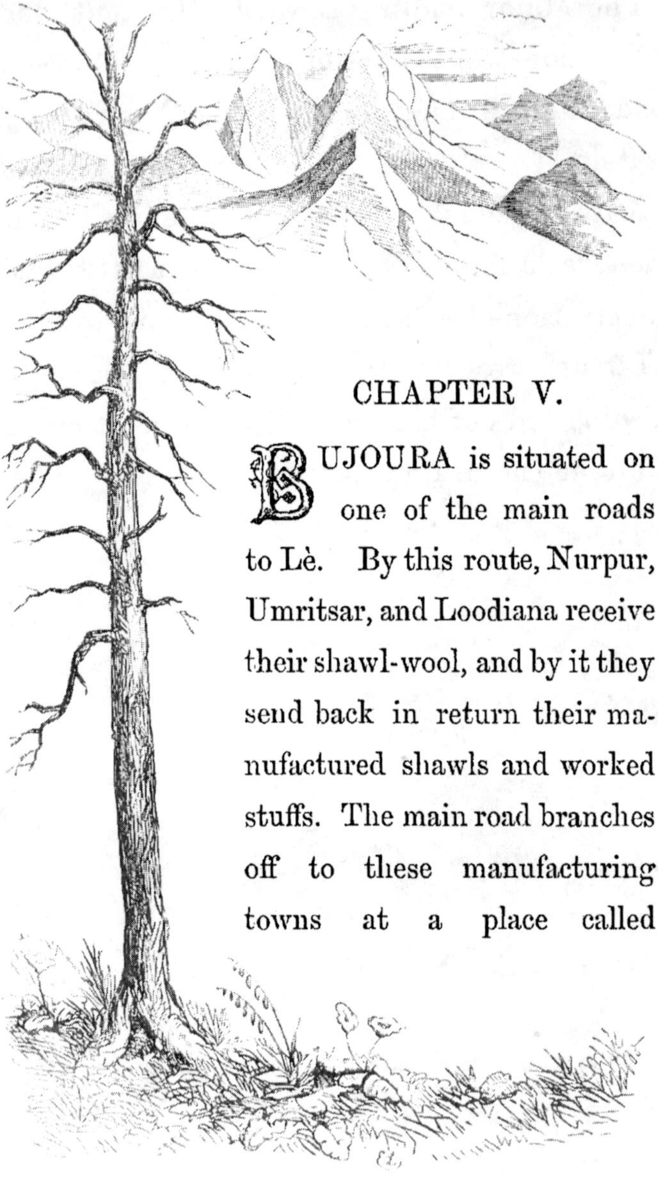

CHAPTER V.

BUJOURA is situated on one of the main roads to Lè. By this route, Nurpur, Umritsar, and Loodiana receive their shawl-wool, and by it they send back in return their manufactured shawls and worked stuffs. The main road branches off to these manufacturing towns at a place called

Mundi* (the market), or Mandinagur (market-city), on the Beas river, about five-and-twenty miles to the south-west of Bujoura.

From Bujoura a march of about nine or ten miles took us to Sultanpore, otherwise called Kulu, and the capital of the province of that name.

The road is a good one, and appears to be kept in good repair. It passes between a youthful avenue of trees, which already afford a grateful shade, and is crossed in two places by branches of the Serbari river, a considerable feeder of the Beas. At the confluence of these two streams, a little higher up the valley, Sultanpore is built, in the angle formed by their uniting waters.

It is not an imposing metropolis, though possessing an upper and a lower town, the former being inhabited mainly by artisans and shopkeepers, while the latter exhibits a few houses of a more pretentious appearance. We were lodged in the lower town, in a sort of square formed by the buildings formerly occupied by the Rajah, in old days, when Kulu possessed one.

I pitched my tent on the greensward which

* *Vide* Cunningham's *Ladak*, page 153.

carpeted the little square; but my companions agreed to pass the night in a sort of alcove, which appeared in its palmy days to have served as a hall of audience, where the Rajah was wont to sit in state and hold his mimic court.

Next morning, however, I found their beds out in the open, and pitiable was the description of their night's un-rest, to the truth of which their blotched faces, half-closed eyes, and swollen arms were silent yet most eloquent witnesses. Directly the lights were out, the quondam hall of audience had swarmed with little visitors, whose appearance was as unwelcome as their entrance was unceremonious. If their object was ejection they certainly succeeded; for soon the beds were ordered out into the verandah—a species of half-measure which was far from satisfying the conquerors, or appeasing their wrath; so orderly a retreat was no adequate acknowledgment of their victorious stings. Bent on a total rout, down swarmed again the insatiable foe, and again were my discomfited friends forced to seek safety in flight.

We made an early start, and breakfasted half-way, our road still following the course of the Beas, which is here confined to a narrow channel; but as we approached our halting-ground, the valley again opened out and gave it elbow room.*

We camped on the right bank of the stream. Opposite us, about half-way up the mountain-side, was a large building, which we were told was the summer residence of the Assistant Commissioner of Kulu.

We were diffident of taking him by storm with so large a party; and, after a council of war, decided on sending a deputation of *one* to wait on him. The most eligible for the office of our ambassador, or representative, was, *facile princeps*, the Photographer, and for many reasons; he was the best dressed! This fact was ascertained beyond a doubt by an inspection of his wardrobe. He possessed a vehicle! (a sort of palanquin, called in the hills a "dandy"), and there-

* One of the five rivers of the Punjab. It is the Hyphasis of the Greeks. From its source in the Rotang Pass to its confluence with the Sutlej at Hariki-Patan, its total length is 350 miles.

fore need not walk, to which ignominious mode of procedure the rest of us were doomed. And over and above certain personal qualifications which eminently fitted him for the task of Mercury, he had the honour of a slight previous acquaintance with the said Assistant Commissioner. So without a dissentient voice he was elected our delegate.

After an elaborate toilette, at which we all assisted, our artist departed, deeply impressed with a sense of the importance of his mission, but bearing himself bravely, like a man who did not shrink from its responsibilities, final instructions ringing in his ears, such as—"Now, mind! we're in a state of abject destitution—no beer! and only one bottle of sherry!!—bread and fresh butter urgently required! for an invalid, you'd better say," roared a voice of stentorian power; "in fact, the smallest alimentary trifle will be gratefully received, and, only you needn't say so, ravenously devoured," &c. &c.

It would require a pen dipped in "imperial purple" to do justice to the triumph of his return. Behold him, seated on a borrowed pony, full of lunch, and the proud consciousness of having done his duty, loud in praise of the courtesy of his host and the urbanity of his hostess, and pointing with a pardonable pride at two slaves who followed him, staggering beneath the weight of creature comforts. It was a very Cornucopia that now poured out its riches on the grass before us.

Next morning brought us tidings of our ponies. They had arrived in Sultanpore, but in so sorry a plight, so battered, bruised, and foot-sore, that we did not order them to follow us; but, sending back for our saddles and bridles, directed the grooms to remain at Sultanpore till their poor charges had recovered from the effects of their mountain travel, and then to proceed by easy marches to Belaspore, on the Sutlej, where we hoped to meet them on our return homewards in October.

We called next day, *en route*, as in duty bound, on our good Samaritans, the Assistant Commissioner and his wife, from whom we gained much valuable information regarding our road; we also petitioned for a repetition of their good offices in favour of our two poor Riflemen, who were doing their best to overtake us.

After a short march of about eight miles we halted at Jug-et-sook, a small village, where is a good-sized bungalow for the accommodation of travellers. Since leaving Sultanpore we had been gradually ascending, and now found ourselves at an elevation of six thousand feet, and one march from the foot of the Rotang Pass.

The character of the country through which we had for the last two days been passing was one of unvarying beauty—the great feature of the landscape being the Beas River, which, with its frequent tributaries, keeps the valley always green. Cultivation is pushed up the slopes of the mountains on either side by means of a series of terraces supported by rough stone walls, having the appearance, at a distance, of gigantic flights of stairs. When the hill-side becomes too steep for agricultural purposes, its green slopes afford abundant pasturage to vast flocks of sheep and goats. At intervals of two and three miles, well-built villages appear, surrounded by orchards of peach, apricot, and walnut trees; the houses are of stone mostly, and two and three stories in height, of which the cattle occupy the ground-floor, while the upper stories house the family.

Soon after leaving Jug-et-sook the valley narrows rapidly; the road, such as it is, ascends at a more perceptible incline; cultivation grows less and less, and the "forest primeval" encroaches more and more. On an eminence to the right were some hot springs, of the existence of which our Hindoo servants were eager to tell us, and also to ask leave to make a pilgrimage to them.

They are looked on as sacred by all religiously-minded Hindoos, and a bath in their waters washes away a multitude of sins. The Hindoos of the hills do not indulge in the diurnal ablutions of the Hindoo of the plains, at least not on a journey; and for our servants to get a good washing was so undoubtedly a *temporal* blessing as far as their masters were concerned, that they easily obtained permission to avail themselves of the *spiritual* benefits attendant on a warm bath.

We here saw the curious ceremony of taking

a god out for a promenade, conducting him, with much pomp, tom-tomming, shouting, and music, to the sacred springs, where offerings are made him of *ghee*—*i.e.*, clarified butter—fine flour, and sugar; and then, for fear, I presume, that these unaccustomed dainties should interfere with his divine digestion, he is taken to a grass-plot hard by, and there danced up and down till his votaries are tired with their exertions, when they once more shoulder the object of their adoration and conduct him back to his deota or temple.

The divinity on this occasion was a strange edifice of scraps of red cloth, feathers, cows'-tails, and other rubbish—a very cheap god, indeed! When new, he could not have cost more than five shillings; and when we saw him he was sadly the worse for his promenades, dancings, and jollifications at the sacred springs. His dilapidated appearance, however, detracted in nothing from the veneration of his worshippers; he was, in their estimation, as good a god as ever.

There was only one spring, which flowed into a small reservoir of cut stone, and was connected with a second reservoir of the same size by a little channel faced with stone.

"A strong smell of sulphuretted hydrogen escaped with the vapour, and the water had the taste of Harrowgate water; but no medicinal qualities are ascribed to it by the natives." So says Moorcroft, who is, I have no doubt, perfectly right; but being myself unacquainted either with the perfume of sulphuretted hydrogen, or with the taste either of this or of Harrowgate water, I cannot take upon myself formally to corroborate his statement.

After leaving the hot spring, we scrambled on by an unfrequented bye-path to the banks of the Beas again, here so dwindled that we forded it without difficulty; and two or three miles more of a gradual ascent brought us to the village of Bourwa, a little beyond which we camped. We had now reached an elevation of fully seven thousand feet; all cultivation had ceased; the pine, the cypress, and the cedar took the place of peach, apricot, and walnut tree; and rugged cliffs and rocky mountain sides met the eye that so lately had rested on the trim enclosures and carefully irrigated fields of the valley.

To our right was the Rotang-ki-joth, or Rotang Pass, which we were to scale on the morrow; we could see but little of it, for thick rain-clouds draped it almost to its feet, and what little we did see looked cold, wet, dreary, and inhospitable. The villagers, on learning our intentions, recommended us to send on as much of our baggage as we could spare at once, and in reply to our somewhat anxious inquiries as to the sort of weather we were likely to find up there, said, "It always rains on the Rotang-ki-joth!"

These birds of ill omen croaked falsely. The morrow broke bright and clear, and we reached the banks of the Chandra river without a drop of rain. It was a stiff walk—a good seventeen miles—in the course of which we ascended *six*, and descended *three* thousand feet.

The tents were struck, and their late occupants were shivering outside in the dim grey twilight ere day broke. We crowded round the smouldering embers of the mighty fire by side of which our servants had bivouacked, gulped down hot cups of coffee or chocolate, and on the dank breath of morn floated lingeringly the fragrance of our morning "weeds." Soon all was packed. One by one the coolies started with their respective loads, and no excuse for loitering round the fire remained. *En avant!*

In front strode the stalwart form of the "Official Friend," closely waited on by his faithful followers, Bujjoo, Nurput, and Noura; the latter worthy I have as yet only mentioned by name, but he deserves a more detailed description. His costume, if nothing else, entitles him to a niche in our portrait gallery. He "wears the jacket red" of a 93rd Highlander, which, though it must have passed through many hands ere it reached those of Noura, still preserves something of its pristine bravery; above this nods a lofty turban, arranged in imitation evidently of the "feather-bonnet."

I can trace no further attempt at Highland costume, however; his nether limbs are clad in a strange medley of rags and tatters, but his step is proud, and his bearing worthy of the "garb of old Gaul," as he shoulders his master's fowling-piece and prepares to follow him.

He was the head-man of the Ladakhis who accompanied us, and on the condition that he kept them in order was permitted to march without a load. Poor Noura!—his language was a most unintelligible jargon, yet he put in his oar on all occasions, and was in his own opinion and that of his Ladakhis, an infallible "Sir oracle" on all subjects.

Bujjoo and Nurput can, when they please, get themselves up in the height of hill dandyism, but on the march they wisely appear in garments more serviceable than costly; to-day they have with them a couple of unladen coolies, and a coil of stout rope, with which the latter will be harnessed to the "Official Friend" as the ascent gets steep, and so aid his upward progress.

Close behind comes our artist, walking stoutly as yet, but within a few yards may be seen his "dandy,"—the palanquin before-mentioned; and the Major—who, with myself, has been loth to leave the fire,—somewhat maliciously wonders how long this unwonted activity will last; the artist is no great pedestrian, and we, it is best to confess at once, are rather proud of our walking powers.

Such the order of our march at starting: our path is a rough and slippery one; to our right roars unseen, at the bottom of a narrow gorge, the Beas, now reduced to the limits of a mere mountain stream, but pent in that confined channel, a formidable torrent still; to our left rises an overhanging cliff, dripping with constant moisture: now up, now down, now turning to the right and now to the left, there is no end to our path's vagaries; at last it debouches on a valley in miniature, not a quarter of a mile broad, and in length but little more; high cliffs crowned with pines shut it in on the right hand and on the left, and from their summits fall frequent cascades, which form into rivulets at the bottom, and intersect the valley. I counted nine of these cascades, and never remember to have seen a more picturesque spot. After crossing the little valley we arrived at the foot of the pass proper.

A rough causeway of stones leads up the ascent;

this is a great assistance to the pedestrian, giving him a firm footing, but it is too steep for cattle; and a winding path stretched away to the right, up which all four-footed wayfarers are driven. This causeway is nearly four miles in length; and when the traveller's foot rests on its topmost slab, he has the satisfaction of knowing that the worst half of his climb is past. The causeway owes its existence to a priest, or *guru*, called Rillat Bhagt, the religious head of an establishment of mendicants."*

The ascent for the next half-mile is much more gradual, and here, with his usual sagacity, had Ali Bux prepared breakfast.

A little to the right of the causeway, and near its summit, is a holy spot, sacred to all the gods in the Hindoo calendar. We were again indebted to the religious zeal of our servants for pointing this out to us; after a good deal of prostration, praying, and offering up of handfuls of flour, and lumps of sugar and ghee, the divinity at last vouchsafed his appearance in the shape of a little serpent about two and a half

* *Vide* Moorcroft, Part I., page 188.

feet long, who wriggled about playfully in the sunshine, which had probably more to do with his leaving his snug hole in the rock than the genuflexions of our followers; their delight, not unmixed with awe, at the reptile's appearance, was unmistakeably genuine—their credulity was no feigned feeling: they believed implicitly in the presence of the supernatural, and their faith was as pure and unsophisticated as its object was foul and erroneous.

They told us that sometimes as many as twenty or thirty of these snakes appear on this spot to the faithful; "but that," added they, naively, "is generally in the middle of the day, when the sun is hot."

The legend runs, that when the gods fled before the might of the Rakis (the Titans of Hindoo mythology), they took refuge for a time in the snows of the Himalayas, and the serpents were placed to guard all the roads to their abode. This was one of the principal outposts of the serpent army, and, from mere force of habit, I suppose, their descendants continue to keep up the routine of guard-mounting, &c.: but they must be sadly degenerate, so trifling a worm as that would have been a ridiculous barrier against triumphant and gigantic Rakis; doubtless they were boa-constrictors in those good old days when the Olympian court was held on the peaks of Kailas; they kept better watch, too, then, it is to be hoped, when ministering spirits went the rounds, for I will swear before any court-martial that the sentry was asleep in his box when we came up, and that when he was aroused from his criminal slumbers, he did not turn out the guard, present *fangs*, or ask for the counter-sign; fancy the lamentations of a veteran serpent, of a *vieille moustache* of the old snake army, could he rise from the dead, over their shortcomings—what a yarn he would spin, commencing, "By Vishnu, sir," and ending confidentially in your ear, with an apoplectic sigh deep-drawn from the bottom of his scaly waistcoat, "it's my belief, sir the service has gone to the devil!"

The legend goes on to say that the gods, invigorated, we will presume, by the bracing Alpine air, or driven to desperation by the *tristesse* of their lonely residence, again took the field, utterly routed the Rakis, and slew them to a giant. The fossils so plentifully strewed over the Sewalik, or lowest ranges of the Himalayas, are the bones of the slain Rakis!!!

This was Bujjoo's story.

Breakfast over, we prepared to breast the hill again. A tedious ascent of about four miles more brought us to the source of the Beas river, which trickles, a feeble streamlet, from beneath a vein of slate, about one hundred feet below the crest of the pass. It is walled round on three sides; and against one of the walls leans a little stone slab, on which is sculptured in rude *alto-relievo* the figure of the river deity, Beas Rishi: withered flowers, the offerings of Hindoo pilgrims, lay strewed about. We, too, made our offering, in the form of a libation, not poured *out* in honour of the river-god, but poured down in honour and for the delectation of ourselves: a nip of whisky at that altitude, and after that climb, was most enjoyable.

About a mile before this we had crossed a small glacier, not more than fifty yards broad, but of great depth. The hardened snow of the surface was discoloured and muddy, and the fissures, of which there were only one or two, were but a few inches in depth. It filled up a ravine in the side of the mountain, and was thawing fast when we passed over it; besides this, we saw only a few patches of snow in sheltered spots.

The pass itself is of a good breadth, and almost level, the ascent on either side becoming less and less steep as it approaches the summit. The surface is wet and spongy, from the number of small springs which ooze from the ground in all directions. The top is marked by a cairn of stones, surmounted by a few sticks, from which rags of cloth flutter. This is erected for the purpose of propitiating the spirit of the mountain, who, to judge from the terrors of his favourite haunt, must be an awful bogie indeed.

A piercingly cold wind blew through this broad gap in the mighty ridge, and clouds obscured the mountains on either side. Moorcroft computes the height of the Rotang Pass as above thirteen thousand three hundred feet; other writers make it a little lower, and call it thirteen thousand.

The Rotang pass crosses what Cunningham* calls the Lahoul range of the Mid-Himalaya, or Pir Panjal chain. The mean height of the *peaks* of this range he computes at eighteen thousand nine hundred and twenty feet; and the mean height of the whole range at close on seventeen thousand feet.

The descent, at first very gradual, soon becomes steep, and in some places almost precipitous. It leads down to the left bank of the Chandra river, which foams along at the bottom with great rapidity. We crossed by a suspension bridge, formed of ropes of birch twigs, about one hundred feet in length; this was the third different description of bridge which had occurred in the few last marches. We had walked across the wooden (*sango* or *shingzam*) bridge, we had been slung over by the rope-bridge (or *Jhula*), we had sat astride on (*deris*) inflated skins, and so been ferried across; but now had come the most ticklish operation of all.

Pendant between two ropes of birch twigs, which stretched across the stream from rude

* *Vide* Cunningham's *Ladak*, page 68.

piers erected on either bank, hung, cradle-like, a continuous hurdle of the same frail material, attached to the ropes above by a sort of open

TWIG BRIDGE.

basket-work; this was the footway, and the ropes above served as balustrades on either side. This footway was further supported by two or three smaller birchen ropes laid side by side beneath it, and stretching across the stream in the same manner as the two upper ropes.

This, when new, is, I dare say, a safe and pleasant way enough of crossing a mountain torrent; but after such a bridge has been trodden on by the traffic of months, and the footway is worn and broken, leaving large gaps through which you can see the swirling flood below; when the basket-work sides have ceased to do their duty, and the roadway swings from side to side, so slight is its connexion with the two main ropes; and when their chief supporters, these guardian banisters, have sunk in the centre by their own weight to nearly a level with the footway itself,—the transit is by no means an easy one, and it requires a cool head and a sure foot to effect it without a certain trepidation.

One hundred feet of closely packed birch rods! What a sight for a "schoolmaster abroad"! He would think it a sad waste of material, I fancy; or rather, what a sight for a schoolboy! so many thousand rods of birch hanging, not in "pickle," but harmlessly pendant, never to be taken down for purposes of salutary discipline or employed in wholesome flagellation!

This rude suspension bridge is called *chuq-zam* by the natives, and is common in many parts of Ladak.

The Chandra rises in the Bara Lacha Pass, and has attained by the time it reaches Koksar a considerable size. The point at which the suspension bridge spanned it was the narrowest that we could see for some miles up and down. At Tandi, about twenty-five miles below Koksar, it receives the waters of the Bhaga river, whose source is also situated in the pass of Bara Lacha. After the confluence of these two rivers the united stream is called *Chandra-Bagha,* or Chenab, and is, next to the Sutlej, the largest of the five great rivers of the Punjab.

The bridge was crossed without an accident —a fact highly satisfactory to the traveller at the time, but perfectly exasperating to the book-maker, to whom the dearth of incident is quite appalling! If somebody had only fallen through, or something belonging to somebody had only tumbled in, what an opportunity for the author! But no! bag and baggage, masters and men, all got across, as I said before, in most provoking safety.

We left the province of Kulu on the other side the river, and were now in that of Lahoul. With a new country shall begin a fresh chapter, but first you shall read, if you have a mind, something staid and statistical, touching trade.

The Chandra river, at Koksar, is the principal obstacle to this line of traffic between the wool-producing countries of the north and the plains, and is so serious a one that it threatens to close it entirely against beasts of burden, for the current is too rapid for them to be swum across in any safety.

The urgent necessity of a good bridge at this point has been frequently urged on the Indian Government, but as yet without avail!

The large admixture of inferior wool with the pure "pushm" (the wool of the shawl-goat), in the shawls manufactured of late at Umritsar, and their consequent depreciation in value, may be mainly attributed to the perils of the passage of the river at Koksar, which deter merchants from taking this line with their merchandize, and induce them to seek a market in Kashmir in preference, notwithstanding the heavy dues levied on all imports by the Maharajah. Supplies of the pure "pushm" of Rudokh, &c., being thus almost entirely cut off by the want of a good bridge at Koksar (for the rest of the route is easy), the Umritsar merchants become dependent on the insufficient quantities smuggled from the Chinese frontier through Kunawur, by paths on which none but lightly-laden sheep and goats, assisted by hardy mountaineers, can travel. But these mountain tracks are only used by a few enterprising adventurers, incited by the fascination of a lawless pursuit, and the large profits accruing from the evasion of the enormous way-dues levied by the Government of Kashmir. The amount of "pushm," therefore, obtainable by their means is but small, and its supply precarious. Hence the shawl merchants of the plains may be said to be driven to adulteration—to the admixture of an inferior description of wool, in order to make their supply of shawls equal the demand.

At present the Governments of Kashmir and China appear to play into each other's hands, the Chinese prohibiting all traffic from their territory save through Ladâk, the territory of the Maharajah, thus enabling the Kashmir ruler to monopolize almost the entire trade, in which he is virtually assisted by the Indian Government, which, as I have shown, has done nothing to facilitate the transit of merchandize by the main route, at present available from the wool-producing countries to Nurpur, Umritsar, and Loodiana, *viá* Koksar.

The Maharajah's profits by this monopoly are so enormous that it is hopeless to attempt to induce him to reduce the duties on Chinese merchandize of his own free will, and until the Indian Government provides another route for the transit of merchandize from China to Hindostan, it is useless to urge on the Chinese Government the repeal of their present prohibition of all export save through Ladâk, because through Ladak it must of necessity come, save in trifling quantities, by the smuggling paths above mentioned.

There being, therefore, this one route only, it seems imperative on the Government of India to render it as practicable a one as it is possible to make it.

A road which should connect Hindostan with China without passing through foreign territory, is of course an immense desideratum. This subject is treated of at some length in the remarks on the New Road to be found in the Appendix.

CROSSING THE TWIG BRIDGE.

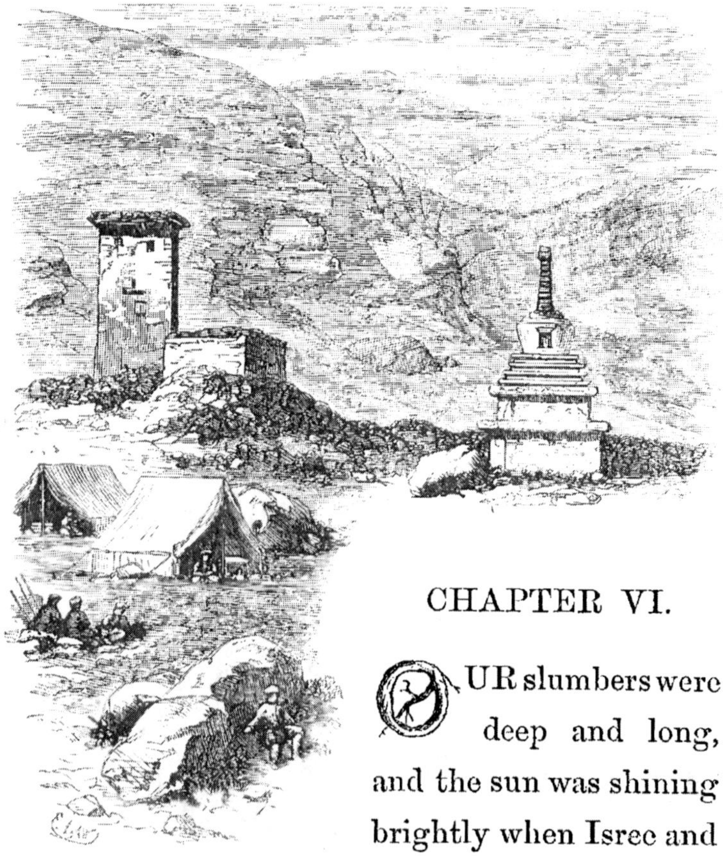

CHAPTER VI.

OUR slumbers were deep and long, and the sun was shining brightly when Isree and a cup of chocolate aroused me from them.

Such a noisy camp as it was! such a Babel of shrill tongues chattering all around one! On questioning Isree, he laconically answered, "Coolie-logue"—*i. e.* "it's only the coolies!" and throwing open the fly of the tent, raised the curtain on as strange a scene as traveller ever saw.

About a hundred women, girls, children, and babies were squabbling, scolding, laughing, joking, talking!—no, not the babies, although they, little innocents! gave tongue too in the only way they could; and a chorus of infantine squalls gave ample evidence of the soundness of their little lungs, greatly, no doubt, to the satisfaction of their *mammas;* not, however, that *they* seemed to care much, their most absorbing pursuit appearing to be examining, lifting, and essaying to carry each package and "khilta" full of baggage, as the servants finished packing them.

They were difficult to please; feminine vanity was, I suspect, at the bottom of it. "The becoming" was doubtless their object; and each one was searching eagerly for a portmanteau that suited her particular style, or a box calculated to show off her figure to advantage. Why not? For what we know, they may study the art of deportment with a view to the graceful carrying of burdens, and a good deal may depend on a load put on with regard to effect. But while meditating thus, I forget that my costume is hardly complete enough to make me presentable to ladies. Those of Lahoul, however, do not appear particular; seated in a semicircle, about a couple of yards from my tent-door, are some five or six, who have evidently set their hearts on carrying my property. They are calculating the probable weight of my luggage, and the owner receives but a small amount of attention from their inquisitive little pig's eyes.

I drop the fly, and modestly retire from their gaze. Soon the sound of a frantic splashing falls on their astonished ears. "Where can it come from?" From "inside the tent?" No; "impossible?" Yes, it does, though! And at last the astounding fact slowly breaks on them—"The Sahib is washing himself! Wa! wa! what an extraordinary Sahib!"

These people wash themselves only once a year, and never wash their clothes.* Jacquemont says, "L'hydrophobie dans un peuple est une affreuse maladie."

"Un jour qu'il faisait moins froid qu'à l'ordinaire, je me deshabillai pour prendre le bain à la mode Indienne, c'est a dire, en me faisant vidée

* *Vide* Cunningham's *Ladak*, page 303.

sur la tête et les épaules un outre pleine d'eau; mais aux éclaboussures de ce petite cascade, la foule des Thibétains pressée autour de moi s'enfuit épouvantée; et depuis ce jour là je me suis toujours délivré de leurs importunités en mettant de faction à la porte de ma misérable petite tente, mon porteur d'eau, ou bisté mussulman, avec sa grand barbe noire, qui était un objet d'admiration pour ces peuplades imberbes, et son outre bien remplie qui excitait leur terreur."

My operations are expeditious; and soon not only is the fly of the tent thrown open, but the tent itself is being struck, while I put the finishing touches to my toilette in the open. It is a most successful performance on my part. Never was audience more attentive, or pantomime more popular; never was act of legerdemain more wonderingly gazed at than the simple process of brushing my hair. The plunging my hands into the basin, and producing them again covered with white lather, caused bewilderment, only to be exceeded by the merriment created by my handling of a tooth-brush. This last novelty was exquisitely funny; and their laughter only ceased when the *properties* were all packed and ready to be pounced on, examined, talked over, lifted, deliberated upon, and finally heaved on the backs of these female porters and walked off with.

These were the strangest specimens of woman-kind it had yet been my lot to meet—at once the most dressy and the ugliest of their sex! Their costume, how shall I describe it? their surpassing ugliness, how portray?

Their hair, of a rusty black, is plaited into a number of tails which reach to the waist, and of which the extremities are collected together and

HEAD-DRESS, LAHOUL WOMEN.

tied under a small bit of mother-of-pearl shell, from which again hang rows of beads and small bells of metal; these jingled as they moved like the bells of a carrier's team, or perhaps still more like that ideal personage of our infancy, to see whom we have so often ridden

> "A cockhorse to Banbury Cross,"

and who has

> "Bells on her fingers, and bells on her toes,
> She shall have music wherever she goes."

I had found the ideal of my infantine imaginings at last!

A band of red cloth or leather, about two or three inches broad, reaches from the forehead back over the crown of the head, and falls as far as the waist. This is studded with rough turquoises, large but ill-shaped, and full of flaws; their colour, too, is green, not blue, and they are of little value. This is the fashionable head-dress! Some (but these may possibly have been suffering from neuralgia) wore flaps of black sheepskin over the ears—*oreilettes,* in fact; and they all of them added as many beads of amber, of mother-of-pearl, and coral, as they could come by. Necklaces of amber, cornelian, coral, and glass (generally the latter), hung round their tawny throats, from which depended rude amulets of silver, nor were armlets and earrings forgotten.

A coarse warm jacket of woollen cloth, a striped petticoat of divers colours, principally blue, red, yellow, and green, and grass shoes or sandals, completed the costume!

A few of them, too, wore undressed sheepskins hanging down over the shoulders, and fastened in front across the breast by skewers—the most primitive of mantles. They all carried small baskets slung at their backs, ready for a load, and most of them had a baby in arms, which, when the able-bodied matron who owned it had decided what baggage she should carry, was handed over to the care of one of the bigger children.

Their sunken features, broad, flat, square visages, were well worthy of their ignoble setting.

The eyes, narrow, small, and twinkling, seemed eternally endeavouring, but in vain, to squint over the prominent cheek-bone, and peep at the flat, broad nose below. The mouth, wide and thick-lipped though it was, was the redeeming feature, for it was generally on the broad grin, and gave an expression of good-humour to the otherwise dull, vacant face.

Their figures, squat, short, and broad, were the reverse of graceful, but they walked away stoutly under burdens which the *men* near Simla would have grumbled at the weight of.

It was quite a *jour de fête* for them, and they had brought their whole family to share in its delights. They were by far the best coolies we had had, were these sturdy, good-humoured ladies of Lahoul.

We marched for about ten miles along the Chandra river to a village called Sisoo. Here we breakfasted under the shade of a little plantation of willows, the only trees we had seen since leaving Koksar.

We changed coolies at this place, and went on after breakfast to Gundla. We pressed on thus quickly with the object of making up for time wasted in short marches in the valley of Sultanpore to allow of our friends, the Riflemen, catching us up; but not having heard from them for some days, we had come to the conclusion that they had grown weary of the long "stern chase," and had returned to Simla.

This province of Lahoul was a strange contrast to that of Kulu; save where the hand of man had been at work, all was bare and barren. We passed several villages *en route*—the houses of stone, plastered with mud, flat-roofed, and two and three stories in height. As in Kulu, the cattle were lodged in the lower story. To those above, the notched stem of a pine-tree formed the only means of access.

Near each village was a carefully-cultivated willow orchard—all pollard trees—and patches of carefully-irrigated barley and buckwheat. In the fields women were working; from the house-tops women stared at us; and women carried our baggage. Where, then, were the men?

We found, on inquiry, that all the able-bodied males pass the summer in transporting merchandize between Ladak, Chumba, and Kulu, and sometimes further, on strong, well-shaped, sure-footed ponies; and not a few, no doubt, spend the summer months in contraband traffic on their own account.

With the ladies, therefore, the summer is a busy time. They have to sow, to reap, and to garner; to stack firewood for the winter on the flat house-top, and look after the "childher," and

LAHOUL WOMAN CARRYING A KHILTA.

last, not least, to carry the baggage of a chance Englishman for a march or two (but this latter occupation is of so rare occurrence that it has all the charms of novelty for them); so that when the good men return home from their travels, they have nothing to do but smoke their pipes, and hybernate through the months of ice and snow in the enjoyment of the good things their helpmate has provided for them.

I write good men in the plural, and help-mate in the singular advisedly, for such is the proportion—two husbands are about the usual allowance to one woman, but there are frequent instances of a much greater number.

Jacquemont writes: "Un trait bien singulier des mœurs Thibètains, que surement vous connaissez, c'est la pluralité des maris. Tous les frères nés d'une même mère n'ont qu'une femme en commun. Il n'arrive jamais que celle-ci ait pour un de ses époux une préférence qui trouble la paix de cette nombreuse famille. Amour et jalousie dans leurs formes les plus grossières sont donc des sentiments inconnus à ce peuple."

Jacquemont was alluding to Thibet proper when he wrote this, but the Botis of Lahoul and Ladak have the same social customs as their more northern brethren, and polyandry and hydrophobia are just as rife among them.

Ponies were procurable in great numbers, but of these, too, nearly all the sires were away with their masters, and only the brood mares and colts had been left at home with the "Missus."

From Gundla we marched to Guruguntal, which is a small village situated near the confluence of the Chandra and the Bhaga rivers; two other villages were in sight at this point—Tandi and Gosha.

The upper story of one of the largest of the houses was devoted to religious purposes. We climbed up to it by steps cut in the stem of a pine-tree laid against the outer wall. There was

PRIMITIVE STAIRCASE.

certainly every excuse for the good people of Guruguntal if they did not very often attend service. The rooms were low-roofed, dark, and small; and in the innermost, lowest, and darkest of all were arranged a few rude images, some flags of China silk curiously worked in hieroglyphic characters, and little tables on which were set offerings of rice and flour in *real* China cups, which made my fingers itch most sacrilegiously. The whole was presided over by a villainous-looking hoary old priest or Lamah,

LAMAH OF GURUGUNTAL.

with sore eyes and the leer of a satyr. As a preacher he could have been anything but popular, and as father confessor still less so. "A very ancient and fish-like smell, a kind of, not of the newest," pervaded the sacred apartments, attributed by the pious, doubtless, to the odours of incense and sanctity, and the *genius loci* himself would have made, properly got up, a perfect Caliban, and looked ready enough "to swear upon that bottle to be true subject" to the first Stephano he might meet with a "full butt of sack."

But breakfast is announced, and we hurry down the primitive staircase to where, under the shade of a pollard willow, our morning repast is spread.

The bread procured from the hospitable Commissioner of Kulu has long since disappeared, and we are again reduced to "chupatties," or unleavened cakes, baked on the spot, and brought in hot and hot; these are made thick or thin, crisp or soft, according to fancy. Sometimes they appeared mighty in circumference, portly in shape, compact in quality, and of a flabby texture—this was a sign that there was not much else to eat; anon they would take the shape of delicate little spongy "*scons*," reminding one of the far distant luxury of a Scotch breakfast; but this was only in times of butter and plenty;

and in general our "chupattie" was of two kinds —a thin crisp wafer, which did duty as bread at dinner; and the luscious, not to say greasy, "pirata," which invariably formed the cereal portion of our breakfast.

The "pirata" is a thin cake of coarse meal, fried in "ghee," or clarified liquid butter, and I seriously recommend the adoption of it to the muffin-men at home.

Pardon this long digression, but being *sine Baccho*, we naturally thought a good deal about Ceres; the fact was, that both Bacchus and John Barleycorn, much as we loved them, were men of too liberal a girth for such a journey as we had before us; we simply could not carry them; and a small store of cognac and "mountain dew" (for medicinal purposes only) was all we could take.

Tea, coffee, chocolate, and "Adam's ale" were our beverages.

From Guruguntal to Kardong was a march of about six miles up the left bank of the Bhaga river.

Kardong was the largest village we saw in

Lahoul, and boasts of a two-roomed building (of which you see the verandah in the sketch); a caravanserai, or resting-place for travellers: we found this empty, and took possession.

The exertions of the inhabitants have made the vicinity of Kardong quite green and fertile in appearance; cultivation is carried to a good height on each side of the valley, but directly irrigation ceases, the bare yellow rock takes its place.

Down below us, on the other side the river, was a low, neat, whitewashed, two-storied building, surrounded by a little enclosure—this was the Moravian mission-house.

The propagation of the gospel among the Kalmuc and Mongol tribes inhabiting the steppes of Russian and Chinese Tartary, has long been a pet project of the Moravian Church.

These tribes constitute two branches of the same family, and speak dialects of the same language.

The formation of the Moravian settlement of Sarepta, on the Wolga, near Czarizin, so far back as the year 1765, afforded the first favour-

VILLAGE OF KARDONG, LAKOUL.

able opportunity for communicating with the tribes who lead a nomadic life on the vast steppes that skirt its banks.

Nothing, however, resulted from this means of intercourse till the year 1801, when a Kalmuc prince sent his son to Sarepta for education; it would seem that the mission made good use of the opening thus given, for in 1808 four girls of the Kirghis tribe of Tartars appear to have been at Sarepta receiving instruction; in 1812, a partial translation of the Bible into the Kalmuc tongue was printed; and in 1815, we find the brethren—*i.e.*, Moravian missionaries—aided by a grant of 300*l.* from the London Missionary Society, actually living among and teaching their doctrines to the Torgutsk and Dorpotsk tribes of the Kalmuc nation at a considerable distance from Sarepta.

The translated portion of Holy Writ was, in 1817, so widely circulated among these people that it became out of print; and in the same year the head Lamah of the Mongols, and the prince of the Chorinian Burats—a Mongol tribe—raised a sum of money, amounting to 550*l.*, to defray the expenses attendant on the translation of the Holy Scriptures into the Mongol dialect; and two men of note and high birth, by name Badma and Nomtu, were dispatched to St. Petersburg to carry out the undertaking.

The chiefs translated the Gospel of St. Matthew into their own dialect under the superintendence of Mr. Schmidt, the Moravian minister at St. Petersburg, and themselves embraced Christianity; and subsequently, the Rev. Messrs. Stallybrass and Swan, of the London Missionary Society, settled in Mongolia, and laboured there many years.

Till 1821 the exertions of the missionaries appear to have been crowned with a partial success; but a reaction took place in that year; and at the instigation of the Lamahs, who naturally dreaded the effects of Moravian teaching, the missionaries, together with their proselytes, amounting in number to twenty-three persons, of both sexes and all ages, were driven out from among the tribes with whom they had lived so long; the little body of fugitives took refuge on an island in the Wolga, near Sarepta.

The Russian Government now interposed, ordered that the converts should be handed over to the Greek Church, forbad further efforts on the part of the Moravians, and so the mission terminated.

Foiled in its praiseworthy exertions in behalf of the hordes of Central Asia from the north, but undismayed, the Moravian Church next determined to endeavour to penetrate to them from the south, *viá* Hindostan and Thibet, and in 1853 missionaries were sent out to Calcutta for this purpose.

Disappointment, however, awaited them: as Russia in the north, so China in the south, barred their further progress; but finding that Budhism prevailed in Lahoul, they decided on commencing the work in that province; here, under the protection of the British flag, would they open their first parallel against heathenism, hoping in time to push their trenches farther and farther: to the north and west, where dwell the tribes their predecessors laboured amongst in the beginning of this century; to the north, east, and south, where the religion of Budh has its head-quarters: meantime, they would be working amongst a kindred people, speaking a dialect of the same tongue, and holding the same creed as those Mongolian tribes whom they hoped one day to reach. This was the scheme to which they devoted their lives—as daring and ambitious as it is simple and earnest.

They accordingly purchased from a native of Kyelang a small plot of ground on which to erect a house. It is worthy of mention that they commenced building in 1857, when the Sepoy mutiny was at its height; but, undaunted by the news of temporary reverses and the prolonged siege of Delhi, they proceeded with their work, having full confidence in the final re-establishment of British supremacy—a confidence, by-the-bye, which was at one time anything but general amongst non-military European residents in India.

In 1859, they found themselves in a position to offer a home to the ladies who have since become their wives; and as is the custom in the mission, three ladies were sent out to aid and comfort them in their voluntary exile. One of their number, the Rev. W. Pagell, proceeded to Calcutta to welcome the fair trio to the shores of India; one of them became his wife at Calcutta; and Mr. and Mrs. Pagell escorted the two remaining adventurous ladies to their future home in the Himalaya.

The missionaries of Lahoul are well acquainted with the Thibetan language, which they speak, read, and write with facility; they have translated into the dialect of the people around them a portion of the New Testament, the "Harmony of the Four Gospels," and some other works of a religious character; these have been printed with the aid of a lithographic press, which they work themselves, and a number of copies have been distributed.

Amongst a people so far removed from civilization, and who have made but little advance since the earliest ages of man, the language is naturally far from being a comprehensive one, and the missionaries found much difficulty in creating words to express the figurative and metaphorical language of Scripture; but their labour has been amply rewarded by finding that their translation fully conveys to the minds of the people the literal meaning of the text.*

They have established a school for both sexes, at which the attendance is yearly increasing; and the girls are taught the simple arts of knitting and needlework by their exemplary helpmates.

As yet they have not met with much success in the shape of actual converts to Christianity; but the people are ready to converse on religious subjects, and take pleasure in tracing the many points of resemblance which exist between our religion and theirs—between Christ and Boodha.†

* Messrs. Huc and Gabet say, "The Thibetan language, essentially religious and mystic, conveys with much clearness and precision all the ideas connected with the human soul and the Divinity."—*Vide Travels in Tartary, Thibet, and China,* page 189.

† One of the many sketches of Budha's origin is, that after living in Heaven as a god for thirty-six million five hundred thousand years, being "desirous of saving men, he came to earth and gave his body to a hungry tiger, and at length, having amassed the necessary amount of virtue, he approached the bosom of his mother on a white elephant. His destined mother, who was wife to the Rajah Ludhoodhana (in Rohilcund), dreams that this elephant filled the universe with light; awaking frightened, she tells the king her dream, and soothsayers being consulted, predict that

This resemblance is at once an assistance and a drawback to the missionary; an assistance, inasmuch as he finds in the educated Budhist a mind prepared to accept the mystery of Incarnation (it is no new doctrine to the believer on Boodh)—and the mere fact of a partial similarity of creed excites a curiosity on the part of the listener to hear more; a drawback, inasmuch as it induces the Budhist to think that Christianity is but another and an inferior form of his own religion, which he feels inclined to tolerate, but never to adopt.

The practical creed of the Budhist is a very moral one; and could he be persuaded that Christ fulfils his idea of a perfect Boodh, and let the name of our Saviour be substituted for that

a child shall be born to her who shall attain either worldly or spiritual greatness."—*Vide Life in Ancient India*, page 255. The legend goes on to say that a child is born, that holy men and sages receive supernatural intelligence of his birth, and, guided by a light in the heavens, find him out and worship him; that the child as he grows older renounces the pleasures of this life, and the temptations of earthly dominion; lives the life of an ascetic, goes alone into a forest, and contends with the powers of darkness, &c. &c.

of Boodh in his creed, it will be found to approximate closely to that of a Christian.*

But upon rich and poor, on the educated and the ignorant alike, the doctrine of the transmigration of souls acts fatally; it is to the Budhist what fatalism is to the Mahommedan. If a Budhist is treated with kindness and benevolence, he sees no cause for gratitude, because he looks upon it all as the result of good works performed by him in a previous state of existence. If, on the other hand, misfortune overtake him, he considers it as a punishment for sins committed by him when existing in another shape.

The vastness of the undertaking—*i.e.*, the conversion of the numerous tribes inhabiting the elevated plains of Central Asia—stands out in prominent contrast with the simple earnestness of the three humble men engaged in it—men who have left home, house, and kindred—who have placed between them and the rest of the world a barrier of snow and ice which is for six months of the year impassable; and who are content to

* *Vide* Prinsep's *Thibet, Tartary, and Mongolia.*

spend their lives among a people alien to them in language, habits, custom, and religion, in the belief that in so doing they are but fulfilling their duty towards God—another duty towards man.

We crossed the river, and paid a visit to the mission next morning *en route.*

Open the little wicket gate! take one short step inside! Presto! pop! You are no longer in Thibet—you are thousands of miles away back in dear old Deutschland!! * * *

One of the Herr Pastors comes forward courteously to greet you (he has been smoking a matutinal pipe in the cool spacious verandah) and asks you in. The sudden transition from dirt and squalor to the scrupulous cleanliness of a German dwelling-house is utterly bewildering. Ere you have recovered your presence of mind you are introduced, first, to a lady who is knitting stockings by the stove; and then to another who is playing with a baby in the window-seat. "The ladies do not speak English," says the Herr Pastor, on which, taking heart of grace, you dive down into the depths of your memory, thence fish up some half-forgotten words of German, and proceed to inform the lady in the window-seat that the baby is a beauteous creature and the image of its mamma—this with a bow which you flatter yourself is rather telling. Alas! poor bungler! the lady of the *knitting-needles* is the mamma!! * * * but this *bévue* causes a laugh, and promotes conversation, and you are quite sorry when it is time to go!

To go? So soon? But not empty handed! A basket of garden peas, of beetroot, and cabbage is hastily packed and pressed on our acceptance. And so, with a kind "God speed you" ringing in their ears, *exeunt* the travellers out of this little Eden of German purity and godliness, into the outer world of heathendom and dirt.

The "Official Friend" had been waited on at Kardong by an influential native, called Tara Chund, whose dwelling was close to our next halting ground. He was the largest landowner in Lahoul, and had lately been granted by the Punjab Government certain magisterial powers, with authority to impose fines, I believe, to the amount of fifty rupees—*i.e.*, 5*l.* Forfeiture to this amount is, in so poor a country, a grievous penalty, and authority to inflict it invested friend Tara with almost supreme power in the barren little principality of which he was potentate.

He was a stout-built, active little man, of about forty, with a good deal of shrewdness in the expression of his ugly face of the true Mongol type.

He accompanied us on the march next day. Our path on leaving the mission house passed through a good deal of cultivation, carefully fenced-in small enclosures, and abundantly irrigated. It then entered an extensive grove of the pencil-cedar, after which it led through a barren country, pleasantly interrupted now and then by the patch of green which invariably surrounded every village or small cluster of houses. After about twelve miles it debouched on a little plain; here, close to a little village, was the paternal mansion of Tara Chund, differing in nothing save in size from the houses of the village; but a few ruined towers showed that once on a time a small fort had stood there.

We came across a manufactory of grass shoes to-day; some half-dozen women seated by the way-side, each with a bundle of grass beside her, were diligently plaiting the frail material into long strips of different degrees of thickness, while others rapidly made it up into sandals.

Of these latter ladies, one was really quite pretty, despite the Mongol type of her features. We could only account for her comeliness by the supposition that we had had the good fortune to see her very shortly after her annual wash.

These shoes are of course very soon worn out, and are never mended, but kicked aside as soon as they cease to defend the feet from the roughness of the path. The road was strewed with cast-off sandals.

We sought the shade of a few pollard willow trees till our tents should arrive. Tara Chund and his sons came and squatted there as well; and a circle of villagers and retainers of the Lahoulee grandee stood at a respectful distance, and looked on at our proceedings with deep interest.

Soon the circle opens out and admits the

passage of a grave procession, headed by an aged Tartar, bearing on high a mighty brass teapot, and followed by others with trays of sweetmeats and spices. These are placed in the midst of us, and Tara Chund proceeds to do the honours. The beverage flowed from the twisted spout in a thick, deep red stream ; it tasted like rich chocolate, and but for a certain greasiness of flavour, this tea *à la Tartare* was very palatable. The teapot is soon empty, and returns for a fresh supply; but the second brew is hardly drinkable, for this time the tea has been seasoned with salt, not sweetened with sugar.

These are the two approved Tartar methods of making tea; the process is the same in both. "It is first made into a strong decoction with soda, then seasoned with salt, or sweetened with sugar, according to fancy, and churned with butter until it acquires the colour and consistency of thick rich cocoa or chocolate."*

We here first met the yâk (*bos grunniens*). The yâk is short, but of immense frame and strength, with a small head, short horns, and

* *Vide* Cunningham's *Ladak*, page 305.

long black hair reaching to the ground, beneath which is a sort of undergrowth of short soft wool. The oxen mostly used in Ladak are hybrids between the yâk and the common cow.

THE YAK.

The progeny, dso or zho, inherits much of the strength and power of endurance of the sire with the docility of the dam, and is used for ploughing, as well as carrying burdens. The milk of the hybrid cow, dsomo or zhomo, is much esteemed.

We made a short march next day to Dartcha, a hamlet of one or two houses, built in the angle formed by the confluence of the Dartcha and Bagha rivers.

The Dartcha flowed in from the left hand at

right angles to the Bagha, which received at this same point a second tributary from the right hand, flowing in also at right angles, so that look which way you would—north, south, east, or west—you had always the distant vista before you of a rocky valley with its mountain stream rushing down—it was a sort of "four cross-roads," in fact, only that these watery ways did not cross, but joining company, flowed away in amicable union towards the south.

At this meeting of the waters a striking land-slip had taken place. A mountain has, as it were, been cut in two—one half remains standing erect, while the other, shivered in pieces by the force of the blow which severed it, lies strewn in quaintly-shaped fragments on the ground it once covered with a graceful slope, and stretches for acres beyond, grovelling at the foot of the mighty cliff it once helped to support, and damming up and changing the course of the stream below.

Curiously enough, when consulting Moorcroft's *Travels*, after my return, on question of distance, I found the following graphic account of this convulsion of nature, which was actually *in progress* when he passed the spot some forty years before:—

"This route has been obstructed for some years by the gradual subsidence of a mountain, which was still in progress, and which we had therefore an opportunity of witnessing. About two-thirds up the acclivity of a mountain about half a mile distant, a little dust was from time to time seen to arise; this presently increased, until an immense cloud spread over and concealed the summit, whilst from underneath it huge blocks of stone were seen rolling and tumbling down the steep. Some of these buried themselves in the ground at the foot of the perpendicular face of the cliff; some slid along the rubbish of previous *débris,* grinding it to powder, and marking their descent by a line of dust; some bounded along with great velocity, and plunged into the river, scattering its waters about in spray. A noise like the pealing of artillery accompanied every considerable fall. In the intervals of a slip, and when the dust was dispersed, the face of the descent was seen broken into ravines, or scored with deep channels, and blackened as if with moisture. About half a mile beyond, and considerably higher than the crumbling mountain, was another, whose top was tufted with snow. It was surrounded by others, lower and of a more friable nature. It appeared to me that the melting of the snows on the principal mountain, and the want of a sufficient vent for the water, was the cause of the rapid decay of the mountains which surrounded; for the water, which in the summer lodges in the fissure and clefts of the latter, becomes frozen again in winter, and in its expansion tears to pieces the surrounding superincumbent rock. Again melting in the summer, it percolates through the loosened soil, and undermining projecting portions of the rock, precipitates them into the valley. As, however, rubbish accumulates on the face and at the foot of the mountain, a fresh barrier and buttress are formed, and the work of destruction is arrested for a season."

It had been arrested for a very long season when we passed, for a few stunted shrubs were growing on the *débris* at the foot of the cliff, and the route which Moorcroft speaks of as being obstructed again took its old line over the masses which were formerly blocked.

Our friend Tara Chund came with us to Darcha, where he and Bujjoo had a busy time of it, for we had now reached the last village of Lahoul, and for the next seven marches must take with us not only coolies, but food and fuel for seven days' consumption.

Koksar is ten thousand feet above the level of the sea; since we left it, we had been gradually ascending, and though the mid-day sun was hotter than ever, the nights were beginning to be very cold. Patches of snow were now frequently visible on the crags around us, and our Mahommedan servants repented them bitterly of ever having come with us; but it was too late to turn back now.

We white men, however, felt stronger and cheerier as the cold became more bracing. The mere sense of height brings with it a strange buoyancy of spirits, an unwonted exhilaration. We were in better condition, too, than when we started; could scale a mountain side without "turning a hair," and calmly look down from dizzy heights from whose edge a fortnight before we should have shrunk back with awe.

LAHOUL WOMEN.

CHAPTER VII.

WE pressed on merrily next day to a camping ground called Patseo, to reach which we had to cross a rude bridge of felled trees and slabs of stone. But it was still early, and though already had Chumpa pitched a tent or two, the "Official Friend" gave the order to strike and pack them, and we were soon *en route* again for Zing-Zing-beer, where, said

Tara Chund, was a good piece of level ground for camping.

The scenery now became wilder at every step,

BRIDGE AT PATSEO.

and we soon entered a rocky valley, which towards its upper end divided into two deep gullies. It was up the right-hand one that we toiled. Mother earth had here clothed herself in armour of proof. Rock, bare rock, rose on either side; rocks, sharp rocks, lay under our feet, and above was a clear blue sky, from which poured fiercely down the rays of the mid-day sun, melting the snow which yet lingered in the clefts of the lofty crags into tiny cascades and rivulets, which came dancing, leaping, sparkling down, delighting in their escape from their icy prison above, while down the gorge, keen and cutting as a knife, drifted a wintry blast fresh from the eternal snows.

A state of things, this, very trying to the complexion. We were all of us pretty well bronzed. Our cheeks had too often been exposed to the fire of an Indian sun in the plains, to care much for its rays at this altitude; but when on our hot, parched skin played this cold wintry breath, the cuticle cracked, peeled, and shrivelled—in fact, surrendered at discretion.

"Take with you lots of biscuits, goggles, and cold cream," was the advice of a celebrated Hill sportsman to me ere I started. And now the two latter stood me in good stead—the goggles to shade my eyes from the glare on the treeless, bladeless rocks, and the cold cream wherewith to anoint my chapped and bleeding face. A mask of crape or cloth is, however, the proper thing to wear.

A mile or two more and the gorge widened. Our path now wound up the left bank of a rapid torrent. It was all "against the collar," and grew steeper and steeper as we advanced. We had commenced the ascent of the Bara Lacha.

We had now been walking some hours, and began to think it high time to halt. "How much farther?" "*Thoree door, maharaj!*" "Only a little way, your Highness!" says Tara Chund. We all knew what this meant. "Thoree door" is equivalent to the Scotch "bittock," and may be any distance, from one mile to five.

On a sudden, turning in the pathway we come upon a young travelling merchant who had passed us in the morning, gazing attentively at some object on the mountain to our left. As we come up, he announces that some "ibex" are feeding up there, and that if the Sahibs like, they can go and shoot them.

We stare, and gaze, and look through field-glasses, but to no purpose; no living thing can we see. But so confident is the fellow that he is right, that he at last persuades the "Official Friend" and myself to place ourselves under his guidance, and, rifle on shoulder, off we start. The torrent to our left we cross by a snow-bridge, and are soon breasting the opposite steep. We have a long climb before us, for to circumvent this wily goat, you must get *above* him; and so for some two thousand feet of sheer ascent we toil on, till our guide motions to us to lie down under a vast fragment of rock that lay half-imbedded in the mountain-side, while, prone on the earth, he wriggles himself forward to peer over the ledge. We wait and wait in breathless suspense; but it is with a downcast look that he returns. The birds have flown; we have had our climb for nothing.

He shows us the place, though, where the ibex had been feeding when he saw them, and proves

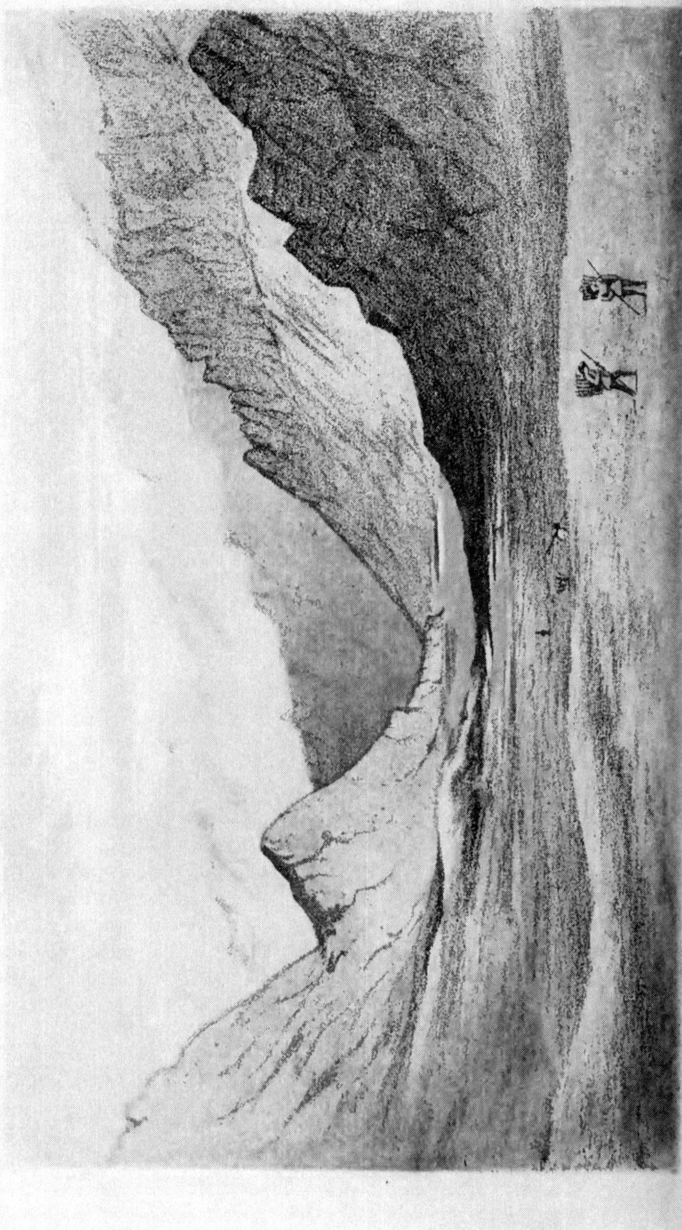

their late presence on the spot by indisputable facts, so we cannot be angry with him.

It is dark ere we reach camp that night, wearier, if not wiser men.

The Thibetan ibex, called "skeen" by the natives, is larger than the ibex of Europe, and equally difficult to approach. Some of our servants disturbed a large number of them who had ventured down the mountain to drink at the torrent that same evening. We set men to watch for them at the same spot next day, but the wary creatures had taken fright, and did not repeat their visit to the stream.

A dâk arrives next morning before we are out of bed. There is a letter from Buckley, who is only three marches behind us, and begs us to wait for him. A halt is ordered in consequence, and scouts are sent in all directions to look out for ibex.

A bleak spot is this Zing-Zing-beer, well worthy of its barbarous appellation. It is situate about half-way up the Bara Lacha Pass, and must be at least fourteen thousand feet above the level of the sea. Our onward path led across a snow-bridge to our left, and so up the pass.

These snow-bridges appeared to be formed by the fall of a petty avalanche from the heights

SNOW BRIDGE.

above into the stream below, which for the instant it dams up, but the current soon finds its way underneath the soft substance without disturbing the surface of it, and continues its course as before. The snow-bed, though thus undermined, does not give way; loose stones and gravel from the mountain-sides roll down and cover it, protecting it from the sun, and it stands for months as good a bridge as man could wish.

The 5th of August passed wearily by—Buckley did not make his appearance—the scouts return without news of game—we turn in early, and sleep dull care away!

"Master! see! big pheasant near to tent; Lord Sahib have gone to shoot." It was Terrear's voice which roused me, and I tumbled out of bed. In another moment two reports, rapidly following each other, told me that the "Official Friend" had fired "right and left." A minute after he passed by my tent-door, triumphant, but very cold and sleepy. He had shot a couple of snow-pheasants, and was going to bed again.

The snow-pheasant is an enormous bird, only found in or near the snow. Its colour, a dubious sort of neutral tint, is hardly distinguishable from the rocks on which it loves to dwell; it rarely flies, trusting to its sturdy legs rather than its pinions for safety when threatened with danger.

We breakfasted in camp an hour or two later. The wild cry of the snow-pheasant came shrilly down from the mountain on our left; it was the mother calling her two chicks, who were, for the best of reasons, deaf to her entreaties. She will not believe that they cannot come to her; and her note, now soft and plaintive, now loud and imperative, sounds near and nearer, till the "Official Friend," seizing his gun, strides off in her direction with bloody intent. Almost at the same moment an excited native rushes in, and says there is another big pheasant quite close, and burning to rival the deeds of the Lord Sahib, the author hurries to the spot.

I find Chumpa shouting, gesticulating, and pointing at something which is running up the mountain-side well out of shot. With fervent blessings on the wretch who had frightened the bird hovering on my lips, I rush off in pursuit, closely followed by Isree, and after a rapid scramble of a few hundred yards, I catch sight of a gigantic pheasant perched on a ledge of rock above me, looking down with a shrewd, "I am a young man from the country" sort of expression, and evidently watching my slow progress with the utmost contempt. I raise my gun for a steady "pot," but at the motion the bird hops down the other side of the rock out of sight, and a minute after I see him continuing his rapid flight far out of range again. Isree and I decide that there is no use following the brute. The exasperating fowl could give us fifty yards in a hundred and beat us up that steep slope, and I retrace my steps in no enviable state of mind, with the pheasant's cry ringing in my ears tauntingly. "But you can't come over me," it said distinctly more than once.

I must say that I thought the "Official Friend" most disagreeable all that forenoon; the airs which he thought proper to give himself on the strength of having shot a long-legged fowl, more like a "cochin china" than a pheasant, were positively revolting, and his affected sneer at my want of success offensive in the last degree.

I confided my sentiments to the Major, who perfectly coincided with me. "Shooting in these

——" (I will omit the adjectives with which he strengthened his very sensible remark), "shooting in these —— hills," said the Major, "is all —— rot!"

Excelsior! Higher and still higher we climb, till filling up a round basin in the solid rock, a clear, deep lake, of about a mile in circumference, meets our view. This is considered to be the source of the Surag-bhaga portion of the Chenab.

We rest awhile on its bank, and talk very pluckily about bathing, but without the slightest intention of committing any such imprudence. Another half-hour's walk brought us to the summit of the pass, sixteen thousand five hundred feet.

It was a beautiful clear day. A long valley stretched away to our right, bounded by heights covered with thick snow; the surface of the ground was wet and spongy like that of the Rotang Pass, but the level space on the top was much more extensive; without exaggeration, it might be called a plain.

I took a hurried sketch of the view, looking back on the track we had passed over, and the photographer took two very successful views. It is probable that photography was never before practised at such an altitude. The result showed how admirably the process is adapted faithfully to represent snowy heights.

After crossing the plain we commenced a gradual descent along the left bank of a rivulet which took its rise on the summit of the pass. Frequent torrents now crossed our path, all flowing into the rivulet on our right, which increased rapidly in volume, till after a mile or two it flowed into a lake of singular stillness, about three miles round.

This lake is called the Yunam lake, and the rivulet which flows out again on the other side is, after his baptism in the lake's yellow waters, called the Yunam river.

We skirted the left bank of this little lake, and then, following the course of the Yunam river, commenced a rapid descent through a very chaos of mighty fragments of red rock, which lay grouped about in grotesque attitudes, and pitched our tents on a small grassy plain which stretched below.

It was on this little plain that we first saw the marmot (*Arctomys Thibetensis*). It was quite a marmot warren. Their call is a peculiar shrill whistle, and they have immense confidence in the fancied celerity with which they can betake themselves to their holes on the approach of danger. They will sit on the mound of earth above their burrow, and let you approach, gun in hand, within ten paces, before they take refuge in it; and even then they pause to utter a warning note—a delay which is fatal to them. We shot two or three: their fur is soft and thick, and of a rich brown, much esteemed by the natives.

At about four o'clock that afternoon Buckley and his friend walked into camp. Their story did not reflect much credit on their forethought. They had wasted precious time at starting, and had latterly pushed on so eagerly that they had outstripped their followers and tired out themselves. Their servants and baggage were still on the other side of the Pass.

A good dinner and a long night's rest did them a "power" of good; and next morning we continued our march. The reader may possibly recollect the bottle of beer so magnanimously left for them at Dilass. They found the bottle; but not one drop of its precious contents was fated to pass their lips. Improvident youths! they did not possess a corkscrew, so seizing the

"DID NOT POSSESS A CORKSCREW."

bottle in feverish haste they proceed to knock its head off; but in his eagerness the headsman fails to hit fairly the slender neck; a clumsy, ill-directed side-stroke smashes the bottle, which, in revenge for such brutal treatment, cuts the bungler's fingers, and the liquor is spilt. This is a fair example of the not wholly undeserved ill-luck that pursued them throughout.

A nine-mile march along a plain about half-a-mile broad brought us to the confines of Lahoul, and we encamped near the left bank of the Lingtee river—the boundary between it and Ladâk. Next day we should enter the territory of the Maharajah of Kashmir.

A storm of wind and dust arose shortly after the tents were pitched, and caused us some inconvenience, for a tent is no protection against dust. This was followed by a small shower of hail, which had the effect of partially laying the dust, and the evening was calm enough.

We delayed starting next day for some hours, in the hope that the baggage of our new comrade would come up: this delay was nearly fatal to the precious boxes containing the camera and other paraphernalia appertaining to photography. Many of these mountain streams, fed as they are almost entirely by the melting of the snow, are easily fordable in the early morning, but later in the day become impassable; and again at night, when the frost checks the thaw caused by the mid-day sun, dwindle back into fordable insignificance.

So it was with the Lingtee river, which we did not cross till nearly eleven o'clock. It was as much as the ponies could do to stem the current; and the coolies were obliged to join hands, and, thus linked together, struggle across in a long chain. The men carrying the photographic boxes were about the centre of the line, and when in mid stream they stumbled and fell prone in the rushing water; the whole line wavered for a moment, then with an effort joining again, minus the two broken links, reeled on to the opposite bank, regardless of the fate of their two fallen comrades, and mindful only of their own safety.

The feelings of our artist at this mishap can be more easily imagined than described. His impassioned gestures—for we could not hear what he said, the roaring of the torrent drowned every other voice (and perhaps this was as well) —attracted the notice of Nurput, Noura, and a few others. The chosen band of Ladakhis, seeing Noura, good at need, about to rush in to the rescue, dropped their loads and ran to the assistance of their leader. Joining hands, the stalwart party reach the fallen wretches, and drag them and their loads by main force to shore. They were only just in time; another minute of immersion and the men would have been drowned, and (which, between you and I, the artist thought of much more consequence) the boxes lost for ever!

Strange to say, nothing was broken, thanks to Terrear's good packing; and thanks to the well-fitting lids of the stout brass-bound boxes, only a few plates got wet; but it was long ere the photographer recovered his wonted equanimity.

The few coolies who yet lingered on the wrong side of the river, preferring toil by land to perils by water, now turned up its bank some two or three miles to where a good bridge promised a secure transit.

We did not see this bridge, but were told that it was a very good one, built and kept in repair by the ruler of Kashmir for the convenience of traders. Our thoughts naturally recurred to Koksar and its wretched bridge of twigs; and we marvelled at the apathy that admitted of a contrast so unfavourable to our rule.

A little farther on we met a large drove of sheep and goats, to the number of five or six hundred, laden with salt, borax, and pushm, bound for Rampoor on the Sutlej. A few Tartar shepherds, and ladies dressed in the height of Thibetan fashion, aided by a few sheep-dogs, were in charge.

We halted for breakfast on the right bank of the Lingtee river: shortly after the path turned suddenly to the right, and ascended by steep zigzags the pass known as the Lung Lacha. We chose as sheltered a position as we could find, about half way up it, and camped.

Shortly after dark arrived the missing baggage —much to the delight of its owners. The servants could not give a good account of themselves; but their woebegone appearance and footsore gait told the true story of their dilatoriness. They all complained more or less of pains in the head and fever: many of our own followers were in the same plight, but we had as yet escaped all the usual ill effects of sojourn at such an altitude.

Next day we completed the ascent of the Lung Lacha (seventeen thousand feet); and descending gradually for some miles along a narrow and in many places very steep defile, we at last crossed and camped on the right bank of a little stream called the Leimgal.

This was a long and weary march, the general character of the scenery being the same as before—rocky valleys overhung by snow-clad crags, and at intervals small plains covered with a scanty vegetation. At starting, the heights on our left took most fantastic forms; they appeared to be composed of sandstone, deeply caverned in all directions, and their summits, broken into castellated shapes, gave the appearance of a long line of lofty battlements.

We met a party of merchants *en route;* they had with them about thirty yâks laden with "churus," and were taking it to Mundi by the *route* we had traversed. We asked them how they intended to cross the Chundra, and they told us that at that point they would have to leave the yâks, place the churus on coolies, and so re-cross the twig bridge into Kulu: a tedious and expensive operation, which would detract greatly from their profits.

These were merchants of a wealthy class, evidently, who did not go beyond Lè, but purchased their goods from the caravans which reach that mart from Yarkand; but during the same march we came across others of a lower class, more like our pedlars, in fact. The complaints of these men related mostly to the heavy duties levied by the Kashmir Maharajah, through his deputy the governor of Lè, and the provisions of the late "Arms Act."

They did not feel the want of their arms in our territory, said they, or even in Ladâk; but on the frontiers of that province, and beyond, they found themselves at the mercy of robbers, whose attacks they were formerly wont to resist with success. The Disarming Act, as far as regards firearms, is no doubt a most wise measure, but it is open to question whether it is an equally wise policy to make it apply so universally as it does to swords and spears as well as to guns and matchlocks, and also to all ranks of men without exception.

The remarkable increase in the number and audacity of wild beasts since the Disarming Act has been enforced, is one great argument against it; wolves, which always abounded in the

Punjab, now positively swarm, and day by day instances occur showing the brute's rapidly growing contempt for his natural sovereign, man, now that his brother man has bereft him of the means of self-defence.

We were now at the foot of the great plain of Kyang, one of the loftiest in the world; it stretches for five-and-thirty miles from the base of the Tung Lung Pass to the heights above the river on whose bank we halted, its breadth varying from two to five miles.

In the summer months it is inhabited by a few shepherds, whose flocks delight to browse on its scanty but nutritious herbage; but ere the approach of winter they leave the wild expanse to its native rulers—the wild horse, the monstrous wild sheep, the hare, and the marmot.

Our sick list is steadily on the increase; poor Buckley is beginning to complain of pains in the head, and the "Official Friend" does not seem "quite the thing," but they both talk confidently of slaying a wild horse on the morrow.

Our camp was a most picturesque one; the tents, pitched on a narrow slip of ground between the stream and the steep mountain-side, gleamed white in the light of the fires which blazed at intervals up the slope, lighting up with their flickering flame the wild faces and forms grouped around them—"Just like a scene at the Princesses," said the Major; and so it was.

The reason of all this festive light and heat was, that the hill-side was covered with the Thibetan furze; this makes capital fuel, and for "this night only" our poor fellows were warm.

A steep ascent of about half a mile brought us next morning on to the plain. Here we separate, and agree to meet again at breakfast in a few hours, at whatever point it might please Ali Bux to give it us.

We have no stirring adventure to tell of at our *rendezvous.* We have all seen wild horses, but none have succeeded in getting within fair rifle-shot of them, and, disgusted with our failures in the stalking line, have returned to seek consolation in breakfast and chat.

The Kyang, or wild horse of Thibet, has been treated with foul calumny by some writers, who insist that he is an ass, not a horse; that he is of the genus *asinus*, not *equus*. Our acquaintance with him was a most distant one; for he very wisely never permitted any one of us to approach near enough to take a certain aim at any vital part, so not wishing merely to wound him, we never fired at all: now this procedure on his part clearly proves him to be *no donkey*. Another fact, and to my mind a very conclusive one, is that he "NEIGHS"—a shrill, clear, defiant "neigh,"—as different from the nasal "bray" of the animal they would liken him to, as his erect and arched neck, and swift, out-stepping trot, differ from the gait and bearing of the "braying" creature.

The hunters of horses pursue their sport later in the day; but when we meet that evening, at the black tents of Rukchin, nothing has been bagged but a few hares, which fell to my gun.

Rukchin is an encampment of Tartar shepherds, whose low tents of black goat's-hair cloth nestle in a little valley which debouches on the plain. A little brook flows down it, and around it the grass grows thick and green amid large clumps of furze; thousands of sheep and goats and a few yâks cover the low hills which bound it, dappled low though they are by frequent broad patches of snow. The flocks are driven down into the valley at night, and a cordon of vigilant

BLACK TENTS OF RUKCHIN.

sheep-dogs, whose baying makes the night hideous, prevents them from straying.

The chief of this little nomad tribe was a tall spare man, well dressed in a long wrapper of thick woollen cloth, confined at the waist by a gay-coloured scarf of Russian silk; on his head was a close-fitting skull-cap of sheepskin, and long boots of Russia-leather clothed his legs to the knees; he was armed with sword and dagger, and carried in his right hand one of the small flail-shaped riding-whips invariably used by the

Tartars; in fact, I had not seen anything so like a Cossack of the Don since I left the Crimea. He turned round, and all resemblance vanished; for, pendant from under the cap of sheepskin hung a long, tapering, glossy, carefully-plaited genuine Chinaman's tail—a tail a mandarin would have been proud of. We now observed that all the "gentle shepherds" wore tails, though none could compare in length and glossiness with the tail of their chief.

Next morning Buckley felt worse, and more of the servants were "down" with fever. Our camp is rapidly becoming a little hospital, and to give the sick people the rest they are so clamorous for, we agree to halt.

Taking a Tartar with me as a guide, I start on an expedition against the hares. Though ignorant of holy writ, this sporting shepherd evidently knows that the "rocks are a refuge for the conies." He took me for three or four miles straight across the plain to where the usual undulating slope of the low hills which hemmed it in was broken into a steep, rocky precipice.

This he proceeds to scale, cautiously peering over every stone, and looking round angrily when my less-practised foot makes a stumble or dislodges a stone. At last he beckons eagerly and points. I can see nothing, but guessing his meaning, and unable to express in pure Thibetan my horror at the notion of shooting a hare sitting, I pick up a stone and throw it in the direction he is indicating; out jumps a fine big fellow from close to where my missile fell; another second and he rolls over with a charge of No. 3 shot in him; after this the Tartar evidently conceives a higher opinion of me, and we have very fair sport, returning much heavier laden than when we started.

Poor Buckley is no better—his head is burning, he says, and he is feverish and weak; so we halt one more day and bag more hares, and, to our delight, in a rocky glen about three miles from camp, some more snow pheasants. Hare soup, roast pheasant, and jugged hare now form a most agreeable change to the *toujours mouton* of our camp dinners.

A Ladakhi calls the hare *ribonq*, or the hill ass, on account of its long ears, and for the same reason wont eat him, thinking him a species of donkey! Poor little hare! it is not *he* that is the ass!! Those we shot were fine plump fellows—quite as large as English hares—and finely flavoured.

On the afternoon of the second day the Major and I rode over the range of hills which bound the plain on the right, to the shores of a large salt lake called the *Tsho Kar*, or White Lake. We saw an immense number of wild fowl, but they were too wary to give us a chance of a shot. They sat pluming themselves within about one hundred yards of the bank, using for toilette-glass the still surface of the lake, and, odd to say, wouldn't "come and be killed."

The water is, to judge from its villanous flavour, highly medicinal; and I recommend it to the faculty as a genuine *Tartar emetic.* A thick saline crust covered the shores of the lake. "Away to the south," said our guide, "is a small fresh-water lake;" but we had not time to test the truth of his story. This piece of fresh water is, however, mentioned by Cunningham,* who says that it flows into the salt-water lake, and he computes the size of the latter at about five miles in length and two and a half in breadth.

* *Vide* Cunningham's *Ladâk*, page 140.

CHAPTER VIII.

ON the 13th August we bade adieu to the gentle shepherds and shepherdesses of the Alpine Arcadia of Rukchin, and slowly wended our way over the plain to the foot of the Tung Lung Pass. I say slowly, for the number of "effectives" in camp was diminishing daily, and nearly all our baggage was carried on slow-stepping yâks. It was a bitterly cold day, for thick clouds obscured the sun, and towards evening snow fell thick.

Many names are added to the sick-list to-night, including that of the "Official Friend," who, in addition to the tortures of headache produced by the rarified atmosphere we had so long been living in, is now suffering from severe intermittent fever.

The climate of this elevated plain is certainly very trying. To a solar heat at noon-day many degrees hotter than in any part of India, succeeds at night a cold so intense that even during the summer months it freezes almost every night. To a day spent, as it were, in the desert of Sahara, succeeds a night of Arctic frigidity.

I more than once, when riding over this plain of Kyang, experienced the delusion of the "mirage." I had ridden far and fast, enticed on and on by the distant gambols of a wild horse, who every now and then would stop, and paw the earth, and gaze wonderingly on the strange creature approaching him; then, tossing his head and neighing shrilly, would vanish in a streak of dust, so rapid was his flight; and when this dust had cleared away, would be seen grazing peaceably half-a-mile off. I give up the vain pursuit, and turn to retrace my steps. It is noon; the sun's rays beat down fiercer and fiercer; my eyeballs ache with the glare, and the whole expanse around me seems to dance and quiver in the fervent heat. Then on the horizon would appear a cool sheet of water. I reason with myself about it, and wrestle and fight against the strange belief in what I know to be a cheat, which still gains ground despite my calmer judgment. I cry aloud that it is a delusion and a snare. But I lie; my heart believes it to be water; and my senses are now revelling in the anticipation of a cool delight which my intellect tells me is unreal; and when the distance that had lent its enchantment to the view was passed, and the cheat was palpable and evident, though mockery was on my tongue, and a sneer on my lips, as I said to them, "Lo! did I not tell ye so?" yet on my too credulous senses disappointment weighed bitterly.

Next morning we mount the Tung Lung Pass, seventeen thousand five hundred feet. It is not a long climb, for we camped at an elevation of at least sixteen thousand feet, but it is very steep; and the snow which fell in the night, and now covers the path to the depth of three or four inches, retards our progress a great deal.

ON THE MARCH.

But the summit once reached we descend rapidly for some miles, and as evening comes on enter the picturesque town of Ghya.

Ghya is built on the left bank of a small stream, which rises in the Tung Lung Pass, and along which our path had wound; the heights bounding the valley on the town side rise in a gradual slope, but from the right bank of the stream rises a mighty precipice of many-coloured rock; there is a deep cleft in this just opposite the town, in which stands a detached cone-shaped rock of considerable height, on the very summit of which is perched a Gonpa, or Boodhist monastery.

To all outward seeming Ghya possesses a most religious population; its suburbs are a mass of saintly edifices, of "manis" and "Tchoktens," of a much more imposing appearance than were the few we had as yet seen in Lahoul. The "manis" are long, low walls of stone, varying from ten or fifteen feet to many furlongs in length; in breadth they are generally about twelve feet, and their summits are covered with flat stones and slates of various shapes and sizes, but all bearing the same inscription—the mystic words,* "*Om mani padmè hom.*" The proper translation of this universal prayer of the Boodhist

* *Vide* Prinsep's *Tibet, Tartary, and Mongolia*, p. 7.

BUDDHIST MONASTERY, "GYA", LADÂK.

is, "O the jewel in the lotus! Amen!" meaning "O Boodh! who hast been absorbed and incorporated in the Divine essence like the jewel-shaped mark in the lotus flower."

These slabs of slate and stone are sold by the Lamahs or priests to the pious, in the same manner as "indulgences" are in the Church of Rome; and mighty indeed is their fancied efficacy, insuring success in all his enterprises to the believing purchaser, who, on receiving his slab of stone, lays it with all due ceremony on the "mani" nearest his village or house. The village mani, therefore, rapidly increases in extent, and from its size a very fair estimate of the prevalence of religious feeling amongst the inhabitants may be calculated. The star of Boodh is setting, to judge from the antiquated appearance and dilapidated state of most of the edifices raised in his honour.

The "Tchoktens" or "offering receptacle," and the "Dungten" or "bone-holder"—for they are of the same shape—are pyramidal structures varying in size; the former are shrines for offerings, the latter monuments or mausolea, erected in memory of some deceased lamah, or grandee. A mythical monster, resembling greatly the fiery dragon that adorns the "old China," so valued by our female relatives of a certain age, is usually painted on the outside.

We observed a change in the dress of the men here; instead of a close-fitting skull-cap, a slouching cap of rough woollen cloth, generally black, was worn; grass shoes, too, had disappeared, and thick soled, square-toed boots, of which, to use an Irishism, "the upper *leathers* were of *felt*," had taken their place, much apparently to the comfort of the wearer; above these, greaves of felt, reaching from the knee downwards, and confined by long garters of black coarse braid, neatly wound round them, helped still further to protect their nether man.

Next morning we were forced to retract the conclusion we had come to the evening before, regarding the serious-mindedness of the good people of Ghya; for, behold! in the midst of our coolies, the raggedest and wretchedest of all, some half-dozen red-robed "lamahs" were squabbling! There must be a great tightness in the "mani" market, but a small demand for the stones with mystic inscriptions, or these holy men would never have been reduced to carrying a heavy portmanteau fifteen miles over rough ground, for the small remuneration of a three-penny bit, and in the service of heretics, too! Verily, the sacerdotal profession must be at a low ebb! We had been studying Mr. Buckle's second volume, and had serious thoughts of delighting him by an account of this priestly degradation.

Let us hope that this augurs well for the future success of our worthy friends at Ryelang.

From Ghya our road followed the rivulet through a deep gorge, in parts so narrow that, to enable travellers to walk dryshod, the path had with some ingenuity been raised on a kind of rude causeway above the waters of the stream, which filled up the bottom of the gorge, and but for this rough engineering would have covered the footway. Anon it opened out, and here little patches of green sward appear lining either bank, and willows droop their graceful boughs in the stream, which here flowed peacefully without a ripple, and—

> "Yellow flowers
> For ever gazed on their own drooping eyes
> Reflected in the crystal calm."

But always on the right hand and on the left rose a rugged barrier of red rock, so lofty and perpendicular that we could see but a narrow strip of the blue sky above. This lasted for some miles, but we did not weary of our lateral prison, after the wide expanse of arid plain we had so lately traversed. The sense of confinement was pleasant; besides, our prison walls were ever varying. Now caverned and mysterious, they seemed to invite the explorer; now solid and impenetrable, they defied escape; and at times up their face, leading from the water's brink to the summit, cut sharp and clear as though with the graver's chisel, would run strange, straight, broad furrows; these were the channels the melting snow of ages had worn for itself through the softer veins of the rock.

The defile widened at last into a small well-cultivated valley, on the left of which, built high on the face of the cliff, was a good sized village called Miru.

Its appearance was most picturesque. There was no attempt at regularity; the laws of street-architecture had been utterly ignored; wherever a ledge of rock afforded a foundation, there stood a flat-roofed, white-washed house, standing out from its red background with cameo-like distinctness. Above all towered the house of the Lamah, and dotted here and there, little pyramidal shrines and monuments relieved the monotony of the flat roofs.

After Miru the valley again narrowed, but the character of its sides changed; they were now composed of a mass of soil with pebbles deeply embedded in it—a "sort of pudding-stone," in fact.* This was soft and fragile, and the narrow defile was all covered with fragments which had become detached, and falling in the stream below made its course wayward and tortuous, and added greatly to the steepness and difficulty of our path.

We halted at Ugshi, a small village situate in

* *Vide* Moorcroft, page 234.

the angle formed by the confluence of the little Glya river and the mighty Indus, which, even at this point, was no inconsiderable stream. It is called the *Sinh-kha-bab,* or Lion's mouth, descended by the Thibetans.

We had, for the last two marches, been rapidly descending, and were now at an elevation of about twelve thousand feet. The change of climate consequent on this difference of altitude had most beneficial effects on our invalids, who vowed that nothing should ever induce them to visit the elevated plains of Rukchin again.

Next day we journeyed for about nine miles along the left bank of the Indus. The first part of our march was over a bare, stony plain, utterly destitute of green, and surrounded by bleak, snow-tipped mountains; it widened out as we advanced, and in the distance began to appear belts of trees, promising from afar off shade and relief from glare and heat. As we approached we could distinguish enclosures carefully planted, gardens, and houses—a pleasant prospect enough, but strikingly suggestive of a Chinese drawing, so strangely formal was the

PANORAMA OF LÊ, FROM THE PALACE ON THE LEFT, TO THE VALLEY OF THE INDUS ON THE RIGHT.

effect of the straight lines of green on a yellow ground, intersecting each other at right angles, that we half doubted the correctness of nature's own perspective. This quaint air of stiffness was caused by the necessity there was of constantly irrigating that parched soil—for rain is almost unknown in Ladâk—and the cultivation clung close to the sides of the watercourses, and ceased altogether when the moisture from the little stream could no longer affect it. So between these grateful rows of verdure "in the barren and dry places where no water was," stretched in its starveling nudity the famished plain again.

Where it got enough to drink, this thirsty soil was by no means ungrateful; for a little further on we saw fields of wheat that seemed to promise an ample harvest; apricots, too, and apples were brought us in basketfuls, the former, however, you must be very hot and tired thoroughly to appreciate, and the latter are only eatable when stewed or baked with an "intolerable deal" of sugar.

We pitched our tents in one of these gardens, and shortly after were waited upon by the

Kahlone of Lè. He was of an old Ladakhi family, and at that time the principal man in the capital; for the Governor, Basti Ram, had grown too old and feeble to hold the reins of Government, and had, some months before, retired to his home in the valley of Kishtawar, there to spend the last days of his active life in peace; a successor had not as yet been appointed by the Maharajah of Kashmir, so this Ladakhi was in the mean time the nominal governor.

THE KAHLONE OF LE AND HIS INTERPRETER.

Kahlone is an old Thibetan title, and in the old days before the Dogra dynasty signified

BUDDHIST MONASTERY NEAR LÉ.

"Prime Minister." Our new friend's "brief authority," however, failed to gain for him much respect from the garrison, for he was accompanied by a Sikh officer, who treated him with but scant courtesy, and took no pains to disguise the fact that he held him in contempt as one of a conquered race.

Our curiosity had been excited by the description of a large monastery in the neighbourhood, and in the afternoon we made a pilgrimage to it. It was about three miles off, up in the recesses of the mountain range to our left. The gorge in which it was situate was completely hid from sight by a projecting promontory of rock which formed a natural screen in front; but this once passed, the convent stood before you. In front and close to you rustled a grove of green poplars, flanked by enormous *tchoktens* and *manis*. On the right of this the path leads; while above, on every projecting piece of rock, were flat-roofed buildings surmounted by square towers, whitewashed for the most part, and painted near the top with broad bands of red. The cliffs above were of immense height, but on every peak, as far as the eye could distinguish, perched these little buildings. We followed the pathway, and, passing under a large gateway, stood in the outer court of the principal edifice, which had been hid from us by the poplar grove.

TCHOKTENS-AMANI, AND LAMASERY IN THE DISTANCE.

It was many-windowed, and several stories in height; square in shape, with an open quadrangle in its centre. At each corner was a square tower, on the top of which flags waved, and strange figures in red robes and mitre-like caps walked solemnly, and blew sonorous, deep-sounding trumpets, and beat drums.

Standing in groups in the courtyard were some sixty or seventy priests, all clothed in long robes of red confined by a red girdle round the waist—their boots even were red. Most were bare-headed, and their hair was either cropped short or clean shaven; but some few wore high hats

A LAMAH.

bulging out towards the top; these, too, were red, and their wearers appeared to be dignitaries of the church.

They told us that the buildings above were

now not occupied, and that they were fast falling into ruin. The fact was it was very cold up there, and these degenerate descendants of the "monks of old" had built for themselves this warmer, grander place of worship down below.

We went over the monastery, which was just the church of Guroogunta1 over again on a larger scale. Amongst other things we were shown with great pride a monster praying wheel; the cylinder was at least ten feet in height and five or six feet in diameter, and it was hard work for two priests to turn it.

These praying cylinders were the great feature of the place, and were of all sizes; the smallest were about the size of humming-tops, and resembled that toy in shape. They are called *chos-khor*, and are carried in the lamah's right hand—the handle being the axis on which they revolve.

They turn at the slightest movement; and as each revolution counts as one prayer, it is easy to carry on an animated conversation, and get through any amount of prayers to Boodh at the same time.

VILLAGE OF BUSQO, LADAK.

Others, a little larger, were placed in shelves along the walls about the height of a man's waist. The pious in passing always give these a twirl. But the most perfect specimen of this business-like way of getting over their spiritual duties practised by the Boodhists of Ladâk, was a little water mill which we noticed a short time after, near a village. The stream turned the mill-wheel, which was nothing more or less than a prayer cylinder, and revolved unceasingly—as long as the stream flowed on, so long would its devotions last. Unlike a "friar of orders grey," apt to fall asleep over his beads, and to shirk the number of *aves* which have been bargained for, this charming little mechanical contrivance never stopped to take breath—never slept—never left off for meals; but prayed continually, and all "free, gratis, for nothing."

He was certainly no fool, whatever else he may have been, who invented the praying wheel!

We now were ushered into the part of the building set apart for Divine service; it was a good-sized room, capable of holding two or three hundred people; cushions were laid across it in parallel rows for the congregation to kneel on; and the officiating priests, to the number of fifteen or twenty, sat in rows on cushions raised a little above the floor.

It was not the time for regular service, but they made no objection to giving us a private performance. The priest who sat on the right opened a book, rang a little bell, and commenced intoning in a low voice—we could distinguish the prayer *Om mani padmè hom* recurring very often. His monotonous chant was soon taken up by the priest next him, and quickly swelled into a regular chorus; then the instruments chimed in, and the clashing of cymbals, the tinkling of triangles, the braying of trumpets, and the roll of drums sounded at intervals. Suddenly, a deep, prolonged roar drowned all other sound; it proceeded from two enormous trumpets that stretched along the floor, the mouths of these instruments and a few feet of their length were alone visible—the performers being seated in a dark cloister beyond. This appeared to be the signal for redoubled exertion, and the intoning, the clashing, the tinkling, the drumming, the braying pealed louder and louder in a rapid *crescendo.* But the pace was too good to last; symptoms of distress were soon apparent after this "grand crash;" and at last, to our great relief, the instruments began to drop off, one by one; then the intoners began to think they had had enough of it, and soon nought but the monotonous mumble of the old lamah on the right was audible, and so the service ended.

I fancy that this was a sort of *extravaganza,* got up for our especial benefit; for apart from the more general points of resemblance, such as the monastic life, the tonsured head, and flowing robes of these people, I could trace but little of that striking similitude in the details of the service to the customs of the Church of Rome which is so insisted on by others. The caricature seemed to me too monstrous to be appreciated; but Jacquemont writes:—

"Le grand lamah de Kanum a la mitré et la crosse épiscopales, il est vetu comme ses prelats; un connaisseur superficiel prendrait, à distance, sa messe Thibétaine et Boudhiste pour une messe romaine du meilleur aloi. Il fait alors vingt génuflexions à divers intervalles, se tourne vers l'autel et vers le peuple tour à tour, agite une sonnette, boit dans un calice d'eau que lui verse un acolyte; il marmonne des patenôtres sur le même air; de tout point c'est une resemblance choquante."* No doubt, had we seen a *grand mass* we should have been equally struck with the resemblance.

Jacquemont goes on to say that Christians of *robust faith* argue from all this that Boodhism is but a corruption of Christianity—an argument which can be maintained on sentimental grounds only. One would think, too, that such "robustly" believing Christians would be slow to admit the possibility of Christianity becoming corrupted to such an extent.

My friend the Major of Cavalry declared that the service we saw performed was exactly like the "Railway Overture," as performed by the Ethiopian Serenaders.

Tea *à la Tartare* was now handed round in China cups, and after it liqueurs were produced in the shape of *chang*. *Chang* is the only

* *Correspondance*, page 260.

spirituous beverage made by the Ladakhis; it owes its being to John Barleycorn, and when distilled is of a pale straw colour. It was not agreeable to the taste, and seemed highly deficient in strength.

We mentioned this latter peculiarity to our Sikh friend, who assured us that it was nevertheless within the bounds of possibility to get most outrageously drunk upon it. This was thought a capital joke by the "Kahlone," and the *one* Lamah who understood a little Hindoostanee. It was soon retailed, with additions of his own no doubt, to his brother priests, and profane laughter shook the walls of Boodh.

The fact is, they are very jolly dogs, these Botis of Ladakh. Every domestic event is with them the signal for merry-making, of which *chang* is the principal feature. The clergy are, as a matter of course, invited to all these feasts, and enjoy themselves (why should they not?) fully as much as the laymen.

We marvelled at the number of these monks, but were told that every family, in which there is more than one son, devotes a member of it to the priesthood. To judge from the appearance of our monkish friends, it is the "fool of the family," I fear, who is generally selected for the holy profession.

Before leaving we were conducted to an out-building, where was a large furnace, above which, embedded in solid masonry, were two monstrous iron caldrons, of great circumference, but rather shallow. "In these," said they, "tea and soup are cooked on grand occasions, and then ladled out through the door to pilgrims, beggars, and others." The door was in two parts; the upper half could be opened for the distribution of the good things, while the other half remained barred against the crowd that besieged it: a buttery-hatch, in fact.

Great expense, they told us, was incurred by this wholesale giving of food, and the smallest subscription towards the convent funds would, they hinted, be, even from the hands of heretics, gratefully accepted.

It was two marches to Lè, a little over twenty miles; but the *Kahlone* promised us as many coolies and ponies as we could possibly want, and we determined to make the double march.

We left Marchalang early, and followed the left bank of the Indus for about ten miles to a village called Chachot, through a valley that increased in width and fertility at every step. Chachot was a long straggling hamlet. The houses were large and well-built, with balconied windows, each standing on its own little piece of farm-land. They were generally whitewashed, and looked quite comfortable, reminding one of an English farm-house. On the roof of each was a thick pile of firewood and dry lucerne for winter use.

We breakfasted in a plantation of poplars arranged in formal rows. We could find but little protection here from the perpendicular rays of the sun, and about noon continued our march. Our path led us now over broad grazing meadows, intersected with wet ditches, which supplied the smaller watercourses used for irrigation. Opposite us, on the other side of the river, built on a rocky eminence, was a castle, flanked by towers and surrounded by a battlemented wall, and at its foot a straggling village reached close up to the walls that protected it; while on the left bank villages, farm-houses, and cultivation grew more and more frequent.

The sun was very powerful, and Buckley, who was still weak, felt it so much that he was obliged to take refuge in a garden and lie down in the shade. He had overrated his powers and was quite knocked up, so we contrived a rude litter for him, and when the sun's rays sank towards the west, had him carried on it into Lè.

The entrance to the capital is very striking. We crossed the Indus by a wooden bridge, then, leaving the river, and turning off towards the mountains, which still hemmed in the valley on either side, passed over the stoniest road in the world to where, in a long low range of rocky hills about two miles from the river, a sudden dip appeared; through this, we were told, we could see Lè.

After passing this range of hills we came on two *manis*, nearly half a mile in length, and flanked by lofty *tchoktens;* then came another narrow, steep, and rocky defile, up which the path wound. It was now quite dark; but the frequent lights, the hum of voices, and the barking of dogs told us we were in Lè at last.

The tents were pitched in a grove of poplar trees on the other side of the city, and here we found our comrades wondering at our non-appearance, and clamorous for dinner.

It was the 17th August, exactly one month since the "official friend" and I rode out of Simla, during which we had crossed the Himalayas and marched at least four hundred miles.

CASTLE AND VILLAGE NEAR LE.

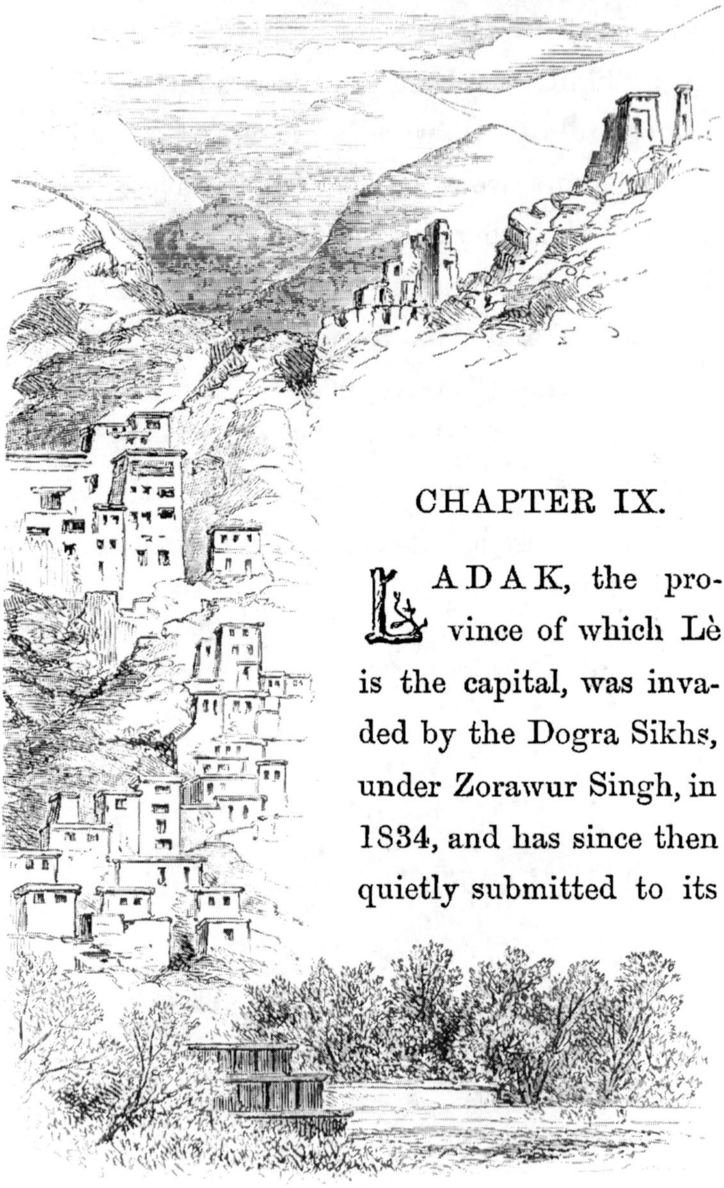

CHAPTER IX.

LADAK, the province of which Lè is the capital, was invaded by the Dogra Sikhs, under Zorawur Singh, in 1834, and has since then quietly submitted to its conquerors. Before this the form of government had been a mild despotism, under rulers who bore the title of Gyalpo. They appear, with but one or two exceptions, to have been men of a weak and indolent character, content to leave the reins of government entirely in the hands of the Kahlone, or prime minister, and as long as the latter kept the royal coffers full, willingly submitting to be a puppet in his hands.

The post of Kahlone is, as we have before observed, still kept up, and held by a Ladakhi; but he is no longer the all-powerful prime minister. All authority, whether real or nominal, is vested in the hands of the Sikh Governor at Lè, who represents his master the Maharajah of Jumnoo.

In the year 1687-88 Ladâk was overrun by the Kalmuck Tartars, and the then Gyalpo, unable to cope with his daring invaders, implored the aid of Kashmir, which at that time formed a part of the great Mogul empire. Thralim Khan, the Governor of Kashmir, referred the Gyalpo's request to Aurungzebe, the emperor, who permitted him to march to the aid of the Gyalpo on the condition that, for the future, Ladâk should pay an annual tribute to Kashmir, and that the Gyalpo himself should become a Mahommedan. These conditions were readily accepted. The Kashmiris routed the Tartar army; and the Gyalpo, donning a green turban as became a true follower of the Prophet, resumed his former life of inglorious ease.

From this date tribute continued to be paid annually to the Kashmir Government, notwithstanding the latter's change of masters, and in 1822 the Ladakhis were so apprehensive of the grasping policy of Runjeet Singh, and so conscious of their own weakness, that, with a view to avert the invasion, which they knew was inevitable by other means, they made a voluntary offer of allegiance to the British Government, and asked Moorcroft, at that time residing in Lè, to become their medium of communication and to forward their tender of submission to Calcutta. Moorcroft, judging that such an offer could not but be acceptable to the Company, readily consented to do so; but not only was the offer declined, but severe censure was passed on Moorcroft for thus meddling in politics.

The invasion, so long dreaded by the Ladakhis, took place in 1834, when the Vuzeer Zorawur Singh was despatched with an army to conquer the province.

The Ladakhis made a protracted resistance, but in the open field were no match for the warlike Sikhs, who treated their opponents with a contempt not unfounded indeed, but which was at times injudicious. The victors followed up each success with energy, but exhibited a want of precaution in the measures they adopted to secure their newly-acquired territory. Forts taken at the point of the sword were left garrisoned by weak detachments, whose very insignificance induced revolt on the part of the partially subjugated people of Ladâk, and it was nearly a year before the Sikh general could call the country his own. The length and rapidity of some of the marches made by the Dogras to check revolt and avenge the massacre of the small garrisons they had left behind them, are almost incredible.

The conquest of Ladâk completed, the ambitious Vuzeer next formed the idea of subjugating the province of Balti, situate to the north-east of Ladâk. Its capital is Skardo; and traditions exist to the effect that it was once called Iskandaria, and that it was one of the cities founded by Alexander the Great. It is watered by the Indus, and the country skirting its banks is more fertile than any part of Ladâk, but the climate in winter is one of great severity. Of this latter fact Zorawur Singh appears to have been unaware, for it was not till towards the close of the year that he commenced his march. At the first intelligence of the advance of the Sikhs, Ahmed Shah, the chief of Balti, prepared for an energetic defence; and, to gain time, broke down the only bridge across the Indus, thus confining the operations of the invading army to the right bank of the river, along which they marched for twenty-five days in the hope of finding a practicable crossing-place. The hope was a vain one. Day after day the Indus rolled his deep and rapid flood along on their left hand, an impassable barrier.

The Sikh troops began to grumble, provisions grew scarce, and, as a climax to their misfortunes, a heavy fall of snow ushered in a winter of unusual severity. Of a force of five thousand men, detached from the main body to collect supplies and reconnoitre, only four hundred men returned to tell a disheartening tale of surprise, discomfiture, and rout, and for fifteen days the Dogra army remained inert, their numbers rapidly thinning by starvation and cold. Discipline was at an end, ruin stared them in the face, and death was busy in their ranks.

The Balti army, camped on the other side the river, or comfortably housed in the villages which lined its bank, rejoicing in the cold which paralysed the Sikhs, watched their invaders dwindling in numbers day by day, content to leave to the elements, which fought so well for them, the glory of their foes' defeat.

But it was fated that in this very severity of cold the shivering Sikhs should find, not only escape from their miseries but the means of victory.

Mehta Basti Ram, one of the chief officers of the expedition, whose resolution seems to have been undaunted by the difficulties which appalled the rest, had watched with daily increasing hope the freezing of the river. "Out of this nettle, danger, we pluck the flower safety," he muttered to himself, or would have muttered had he ever read Shakespeare; and one dark night, with only one follower, he examined the ice up and down for miles, while a small party of about forty Sikhs, whom his courage had inspired with some sparks of their former energy, kept up a smart fire on the Balti people, with a view to distract their attention from the daring explorer.

After an anxious search, and many a perilous trial, Basti Ram found a place where the river was completely frozen across. The ice at the sides was firm and strong, but that in the centre too weak to bear a man's weight; but Basti Ram was as full of resources as he was of pluck. Hastening back to his firing party, he directed them to cut down trees, and carry them to the river bank; these, laid across the weak parts of the ice, soon rendered the whole passable.

Ere morning dawned our hero had crossed the Indus with his little party, now reduced to twelve men; for ten, exhausted by their night's work, lay helpless on the ground; and eighteen others were so benumbed with cold and exposure, that they could neither move through the snow nor handle their arms.

The Balti people, perceiving how insignificant in numbers was this resolute little band, moved down rapidly to attack them; but these thirteen men held their own until Zorawur Singh could arouse a few hundred of his soldiers from their torpor, and cross to their assistance.

A general action followed, in which the men of Balti were defeated, with a loss of three hundred killed and wounded. The loss of the Sikhs in this affair was not more than forty killed and wounded, but the casualties caused by the frost were much more numerous.

Zorawur Singh followed up his victory with energy, and pursued the enemy for nine miles, slaughtering many with the edge of that cruel tulwar the Sikhs so well know how to use on a flying foe.

No further opposition was made to their advance; the fort of Skardo was surrendered after a mere show of resistance; and thus was Balti added to the possessions of the Maharajah of Jumnoo.

The provinces of Rudok and Garo, abounding in shawl wool, and studded with richly-endowed monasteries, next tempted the ambition and cupidity of the Vuzeer. The fear of exciting the wrath of the Chinese Government, to which these countries are subject, did not deter him from carrying out his schemes of unscrupulous aggrandizement; and in 1841 he marched an army of five thousand men up the valley of the Indus.

Rudok and Garo submitted almost without a blow; and the conquerors appear to have spread themselves over the country in small and widely-scattered detachments. Zorawur Singh established his head-quarters on the Sutlej, near its rise in the sacred lakes of Manasravara. Basti Ram was stationed close to the Nepaul frontier, while an officer named Ghulam Khan was specially deputed to plunder the monasteries and desecrate the temples of Boodha.

But a day of retribution was at hand! Intelligence of the approach of a Chinese army, ten thousand strong, soon reached Zorawur Singh; but flushed with his successes, the Sikh General had learned to despise his enemies, and he had the audacity to despatch a small force of about three hundred men to check the advance of the Lhassan army. This handful of men was cut to pieces, and hardly a man escaped. A similar fate attended a second force of six hundred men, sent for the same purpose; on which, collecting all his available troops, Zorawur Singh marched in person to attack them.

The two armies met, and kept up a desultory fire on each other for two days without much loss on either side; but on the morning of the third day the Sikh General was struck by a ball, and fell from his horse. Taking advantage of the confusion caused by the fall of the Dogra leader, the Chinese charged and put the Sikh army to flight. The rout was complete, and the slaughter a most bloody one: with but few exceptions those who escaped the sword of the Chinamen fell victims to the pitiless frost.

But I cannot wind up my brief narrative without saying a word or two of excuse for what may seem the pusillanimity of the Sikhs on this occasion. We must remember that it was mid-winter; that their battle-ground was at least fifteen thousand feet above the level of the sea; that the temperature, even in mid-day, was never above freezing point—serious disadvantages, these, for Indians to fight under! while their foes, numerically much superior, felt the cold no more than their opponents would have felt the oppressiveness of an Indian sun.

Our plucky friend Basti Ram, thinking that on this occasion "discretion was the better part of valour," and that he "that fights and runs away, may live to fight another day," escaped over the snows of the Himalayas into the British district of Kumaon. Let us not blame him. He had well won his spurs, and received substantial rewards for his Indus exploit; and if urged to avenge his late leader's fall, might have said with that knowing soldier of Rome, "*Ibit eo, quo vis, qui zonam perdidit.*" Besides, he had no choice in the matter: any other course for him and his little garrison to take would have been madness.

He afterwards succeeded Zorawur Singh in

the Governorship of Ladâk; and, taking warning by his predecessor's fate, attempted no conquests, but abode quietly in his capital, enriching himself by the arts of peace, and, his calumniators say, extortion, till feeling the hand of Time pressing heavily on him, and conscious of the infirmities of age, he begged permission to resign office, and pass the remainder of his days in retirement. Peace be with him! Were that passage of the Indus his only exploit, he has deserved well of his country.

CHAPTER X.

OUR camp at Lè was pleasantly situated; a thick grove of poplars shaded us from the sun, and while we were not sufficiently far from the city to make a shopping expedition a weary walk, we were not near enough to run the risk of being mobbed by inquisitive townsfolk.

We spent three days at Lè, more for the

sake of our servants, who were weary and footsore, and our invalids, who sorely wanted rest, than for sight-seeing purposes.

There is but little to interest the traveller in the capital of Ladâk; from a distance, the city has an imposing appearance, which it owes entirely to the palace, which, built on a slight eminence, possesses a front of two hundred and fifty feet, and is seven stories in height. It towers "like a tall bully" over the cluster of squalid houses and dirty lanes at its foot, an apt symbol of the Dogra rule; its white walls, too, have a slight slant inwards from base to summit, as if they shrank back with aristocratic disdain from contact with the plebeian huts below.

Proud though it be, it however submits to the supremacy of the church; for high above it, on the summit of a rocky mountain, is a monastery, or lamasery, as Huc more correctly terms them, with its painted battlements and flags. In the centre of the city is a large open marketplace: this on the arrival of a khafila, *i.e.*, caravan from Yarkund and Persia, must be a busy scene. One of these was daily expected while we were there, but on the third morning of our stay it was still some marches off, and we could not afford time to linger there longer.

LE FROM THE MARKET-PLACE.

I can therefore only speak of Lè as it appeared in an interval of stagnation, and there certainly was about as great a dearth of all stir or movement in its streets as in a city of the dead; no need here of Policeman X, such a functionary would soon pine away for want of employment, and even the words "Muv on," that shibboleth of his class, would from constant disuse, slip from his memory.

The absence of the Governor, too, no doubt added greatly to the deserted appearance of the place, for even the palace was empty.

The city is situate in a plain of small extent which slopes down in a gradual fall to the banks of Sinh-kha-bab. Rocky hills about two thousand feet above the level of the city itself, surround it on all sides except the south-west, where there is a good deal of cultivation on either bank of the little Lè rivulet, which falls into the Indus about three or four miles from the city. On this rivulet is a small fort, built by the Dogra invaders, and garrisoned with three hundred men; it commands the approach to the city from Kashmir, and its situation on the bank of the rivulet ensures a supply of water.

The walls, from the bottom of the ditch, which

is scarped and about fifteen feet in breadth as well as in depth, are about thirty feet in height, built of large sun-dried bricks. The barracks for the garrison are inside the fort, and the roof of these buildings forms the *terre-plein* of these ramparts. Its armament consists of four guns of small calibre, and appeared to be in good order.

The city of Lè itself is enclosed by a low wall, with square towers at intervals, which stretches up the slope of the hills; this appears in Moorcroft's time to have been in good order, but it is now in many places demolished and ruinous, and houses have been built outside it.

Plantations of poplar surround the city on all sides; outside these again are *tchoktens* and *manis* without number, extending far up the rocky rises of the encircling hills.

The streets and lanes open out from either side of the market-place, and are narrow and tortuous, forming a most intricate labyrinth. The houses are built generally of bricks burnt in the sun, and are sometimes three stories in height; the roofs are flat, formed of poles of poplar laid across, resting on the outer wall; above these, a sort of hurdle of osiers gives support to a layer of straw and earth, a species of covering but badly calculated to keep out rain.

The houses are whitewashed on the outside, but the original colour of the material is not interfered with within doors, where a good dirt colour is no doubt the most appropriate tint. Moorcroft spent a winter here, and informs us, that "the floor serves for chair, table, and bed, and is not unfrequently shared with sheep and goats, and swarms with more objectionable tenants."

A rude sort of shutter does duty both as door and window, and chimneys are unknown. The interior economy of the palace itself was in no way superior to that of its humbler neighbours; it is a "whited sepulchre," a mighty sham.

The dress of the people, *i.e.*, Ladakhis *pur sang,* differed in nothing from that of those of Lahoul save in the costliness of the material, but of these noble Thibetans we saw but few. Kashmiris, on the contrary, were there in plenty, clad in the long drab wrapper and skull-cap with turban, or skull-cap without turban, accordingly as the wearer was rich or poor, smart or slovenly. Between them and the Ladakhi ladies a mixed race has sprung up called Argands or Argons, who have the white parchmenty complexion of the sires, but are a degenerate race in all points save rascality and ugliness; in these qualities they surpass even the parent stock.

LADAKHIS.

We observed many of the women with their faces smeared with a preparation that left dark stains on the skin, and gave it the appearance of having been varnished; this preparation would seem to be the pulp of some fruit, for a number of small seeds remain glued to the cheek after the operation.

Moorcroft mentions this custom, and gives as a reason for its use, that it is thought to improve the beauty of the female countenance. But it answers so nearly to the description given by the Reverend Messrs. Huc and Gabet of a portion of the toilet of the ladies of Lhassa, not willingly adopted by them as an enhancer of their charms, but enforced by a stern moralist for a very different reason, that I am inclined to think Moorcroft mistaken in his conclusion.

It appears from the account of those two enterprising Frenchmen, that once upon a time, some two hundred years ago, the ladies of Lhassa were so charming and irresistible, that the men of that age were unable to keep them in obedience under them. Petticoat influence spread more and more, till even the holy lamahs were affected by it; in a word, the *chronique scandaleuse* of that period was a very voluminous one. With a view to check this increasing disregard for *les convenances*, the then ruler, a rigid and austere man, decreed that for the future no woman should appear in public without first smearing her face "with a sort of black glutinous varnish, not unlike currant jelly;" that the fair sex should take as much pains to make their faces repulsive, as they had before taken to adorn them.

Strange to say, this edict, so galling to female ideas, was carried out in its integrity, and its observance is to this day strictly attended to in the streets of Lhassa by all ladies with any regard for their reputation.

The Thibetans say that this inhuman order on the part of the King had the desired effect. Features the most winning, when seen through a smudge of currant jelly, failed to seduce; "sweets to the sweet superfluous," and the superfluity palled; the tempter ceased to be tempting, and by this unworthy artifice the "lords of creation" regained their supremacy over its ladies. But Messrs. Huc and Gabet, though not in a position to affirm the contrary with decision, give us to understand that if the morals of the good people of Lhassa were more lax in former days than they are now, they must have been *very bad indeed.*

It was at Lè that we first heard the good news of the existence of a missing note-book of the adventurous Adolphe Schlagentweit. An account of the steps taken to secure it and their result will be found in the Appendix.

I will here quote only one paragraph, which appears to me deserving of attention:—"Dr. Hurkishen states that he received a letter from Mr. A. Schlagentweit, dated the 14th June, 1857, in which he mentions having sent two dâk parcels for transmission to Kangra (see printed circular). The parcels never came to hand; nor does any inquiry appear to have been made respecting their fate. This is unfortunate; even now it is not too late.—(Signed) W. Hay."

Now the book recovered by us is Schlagentweit's journal *from* the 14th June, 1857, containing his notes and observations from the date on which he despatched these two parcels (full of precious matter, which, poor fellow, he had doubtless every reason to believe would reach its destination in safety) up to the day of his death.

But they "never came to hand, nor does any inquiry appear to have been made respecting their fate."

This plain statement of facts needs no comment; let us hope that "even now it is not too late," as Lord W. Hay observes.

The recovery of the volume which has been secured seemed improbable, if not impossible. Adolphe's brothers even seem to have despaired of ever seeing it; yet it has "turned up" by a strange chance—rescued from the snuffy fingers of a Kashgar tobacconist by a man who had but a vague notion of its value: it belonged to a murdered sahib—that was all he knew. And I feel sure that an authoritative search through the villages along the route which the two missing parcels should have taken, would result successfully. Has the Dead-Parcel Office at Kangra been rummaged?

I am happy to be able to add that a letter from the two surviving brothers, acknowledging with joyful thanks the receipt of Adolphe Schlagentweit's last note-book has reached Simla.

Mirza Abdul Wudud, who has rendered unknowingly so great a service to the world of science, was a man whose appearance would have secured him honourable notice in any country, amongst any people. His turban was a miracle of art, and when (as often occurred when the march was long and the sun oppressive) he used to doff its graceful folds, and seem to court

MIRZA ABDUL WUDUD.

"sudden death" by exposing his shaven head, covered merely with a thin skull-cap, to its rays, it was observable that to wear a turban properly you must be, as it were, "to the manner born;" you must possess a cranium lofty, and tapering almost to a point, a cone-shaped skull, round which to wreathe its intricate drapery.

The grave, philosophical calm of his features, the long sleepy eye, the slow dignity of his gait (about one mile and a half an hour,—he never moved faster), his tall, portly figure and commanding presence, his comparatively fair complexion—for I have seen many a British soldier with, thanks to an Indian sun, a darker cheek than his—his self-possessed demeanour, never flurried, never insolent, never obsequious, his language—for he only spoke Persian—distinguished him most markedly from amongst the other followers of our camp. He marched with us as far as Simla, and after receiving the reward granted him by Government, he bade us a courteous farewell, and started "to see India," so he said.

He did not smoke, but was the most inveterate snuff-taker I ever met; and to this habit he undoubtedly owes his rupees five hundred. And to it is the world of letters indebted for the recovery of Adolphe Schlagentweit's last journal—leading him, as it did, straight to the shop of the dealer in snuff, who was unwittingly the possessor of such a treasure.

When questioned as to the disguise he had adopted in the wild countries of Central Asia—that of a hakeem or physician—he, without changing a muscle of his face, told us that he was guiltless of all medicinal or surgical knowledge, but that his practice had been an extended one, even lucrative, amongst those barbarous and ignorant races; but as he came further south, he found his practice decline, his patients grow suspicious, his gains apocryphal. Hence his destitute state when he accosted the "official friend" at Lè with the air of a deposed monarch rather than that of a wandering mendicant.

It was from him that we first learnt of the newly established Russian settlement and manufactory at Kashgar.

The skull which accompanied the note-book has been proved by unmistakeable marks *not* to be that of a European.

It is strange that the two most comprehensive scientific works on India and the neighbouring countries should be the result of the labours and researches of foreigners—I allude to Jacquemont and the Schlagentweits. And still stranger is it that the collections, mineral and vegetable, made by the talented trio of Germans should be at this moment in the Museum of *Berlin*, and not in that of the East India House, although the expense incurred by the Indian Government in behalf of these German *savants* has been computed at near 30,000*l.*, and that incurred by Prussia *nil*.

This, let me add, is no fault of the Messrs. Schlagentweit; they appear to have performed their task ably and zealously, leaving the bones of one of their number in India, a victim to his sense of duty and spirit of adventure. The fault lies entirely at the door of those who organized the expedition; and it is a fault the more to be regretted, seeing that on more than one occasion has this lavish expenditure been quoted by the India House as an excuse for not aiding by pecuniary advances the scientific labours of others, our own countrymen.

It seems, too, matter of regret that foreigners, however able, should have been selected for a task for which the ranks of the then Company's army contained so many admirably suited men, officers in the scientific branches of the service, learned and adventurous, whose habits of life, knowledge of native character, and tried ability were sufficient fully to outweigh the pretensions even of *protégés* of the great Humboldt himself.

At Lè we were joined by a sleek, well-dressed native, who brought to the "official friend" a letter of greeting from Rumbeer Singh, the Maharajah of Jumnoo, in whose territories we now were, and informing him that the sleek, well-whiskered moonshee, the bearer of the flowery epistle, written on vellum, stamped with sprigs of gold, and encased in a *kincob* cover, would attend him throughout his journeyings, and that a small guard of soldiers would also accompany us.

While the invalids were slowly gaining strength, and the photographer was busily taking views, the Major and myself were—to speak veraciously—bored to death. We inspected the stores of some Punjab merchants who were awaiting the arrival of the Khafila, but there was but little to tempt us to open our purse-strings. We hunted everywhere for turquoises, but could find none except the large, rough, green-hued, deeply flawed stones worn on the women's lappets; of these we bought a few at a rupee apiece. We rummaged all the shops, saw everything, whether it was worth seeing or not; and as a last resource, on the evening of the second day, caused it to be announced that the sahibs were anxious to buy ponies.

Next morning we were beset by horsedealers. The Yarkand ponies are fine powerful animals; they usually arrive at Lè sadly out of condition, footsore skeletons with sore backs, for they are generally overladen, and the route from Yarkand is a trying one, passing as it does over the Karakorem range.

The Yarkand merchants never take them back, but sell them for what they will fetch; the large profits on their merchandize fully compensating for any loss they may sustain in horseflesh.

The third day of our stay at Lè was devoted to selecting *montures* from the numerous animals brought for sale, and, as it turned out, we had every reason to be satisfied with our purchases.

The Lè horsedealers are no unworthy members of that knowing fraternity. They invariably asked three times the price they were prepared to take, and probably six times the actual value of the beast; and after you had concluded what you in your innocence thought a capital bargain, and paid your money, the rascals would say with a roguish leer, "Lor' bless ye, sir; why I'd a taken 'arf that sum for the 'oss;" or words to that effect.

Next day we left the capital of Ladâk without a regret.

"Hey! for Kashmir!" Our journey thither shall be told in the next chapter.

THE PIPE.

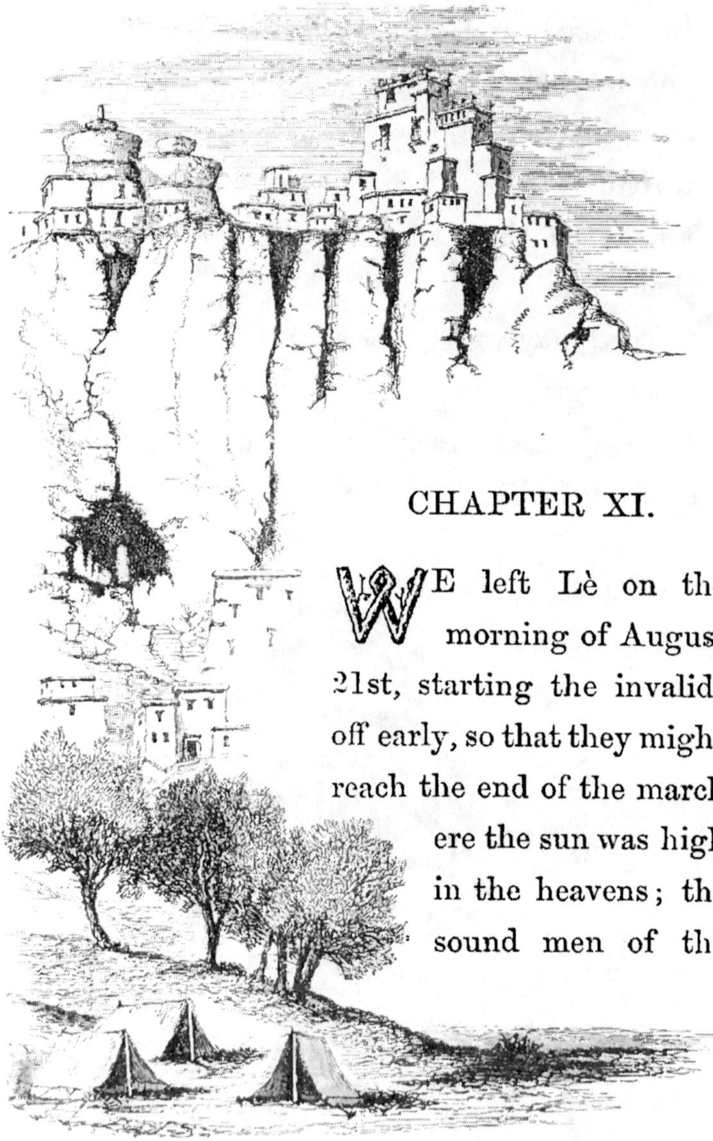

CHAPTER XI.

WE left Lè on the morning of August 21st, starting the invalids off early, so that they might reach the end of the march ere the sun was high in the heavens; the sound men of the party dallied with sleep a little longer, postponing their departure to a more fitting and gentleman-like hour, when they leisurely followed.

Our road led us along the little Lè rivulet, past the fort, down to the Indus, and for some little distance followed the windings of its right bank; then climbing a sandy hill up to the right, it traversed a weary plain of rock and sand for a few miles, when bethinking it of the green margin of the river it had so foolishly deserted, it turned suddenly to the left, down a steep ravine, which, after turnings and twistings without number, each of which it led us to believe was the last, finally debouched on a narrow plain skirting the river bank. A little further on, a small plantation of poplars tempted us from the path by promises of shade, and here we found our *avant garde* stretched on the ground, each with a little mountain of apricots and apples near him, rapidly disappearing before the vigorous attacks of a convalescent's appetite. A mighty jar of fresh milk, no longer full, was being passed round with a pertinacity that threatened soon to empty it; and, as we approached, they announced, with their mouths full, their firm determination not to stir one inch further that day.

We were without difficulty persuaded to concur in this resolve, so a halt was ordered.

From our pleasant poplar grove we marched next day to Nikra, about twelve miles, along a tolerably level road, passing several villages, cultivated fields, and orchards of apricot and apple-trees. Of the villages, Bazgo is the only one worth mentioning; it must at one time have been a place of some note. The old town was built on the crest of a cliff of red sandstone, but was now quite deserted and rapidly falling into ruin. A modern Bazgo had sprung up at its foot.

I was more than once vividly reminded of the scenery of the south of the Crimea as we marched through the Indus valley. There was the same abrupt contrast between luxuriant vegetation and bare rock constantly recurring. The villages were similarly situated, and even the inhabitants resembled greatly in dress and appearance their Crim Tartar brethren.

At Nikra we encamped under a clump of pollard willow-trees, which formed a little oasis on the bare brow of a hill overlooking the river. Here our friend the Kahlone of Lè reappeared. He had just been apprised of the approach from Kashmir of the newly-appointed Governor of Ladâk, and had ridden out with a small escort to meet His Excellency and conduct him with all due honours to his capital.

From Nikra to Hemis was a short march of about ten miles, during which we wandered away from the Indus over a succession of low hills, divided by small glens and valleys, each of which was watered by a little rivulet which ran swiftly down its centre, eager to cast its mite into the all-absorbing "Sinh-ka-bab." We finally pitched our tents about three miles from the great river, under a grove of the sacred "Shukpa," or pencil cedar.

We were stretched on the grass beneath the shade of these venerable trees, listlessly dreaming away the hours, when a sudden commotion in camp roused us from our reverie.

The Kahlone called for his pony, clambered up

into the high-peaked saddle, and rode off at speed. Soon the tramp of advancing cavalry fell on our ears, and, winding down the steep defile in front of us, a brilliant cavalcade of about a hundred horsemen, armed with sword and spear, wretchedly mounted, but most gaily caparisoned, appeared in sight. In the midst of the troop, attended by a select staff of Sikh officers, rode the new governor. He was a nephew of that Basti Ram of whom I have before made honourable mention.

The procession passed our little encampment without halting, and went on to a village at some little distance near the river-bank, where accommodation had been prepared for the representative of the Kashmir Government.

An hour or two afterwards two coolies, the one bearing the bedding, the other the wardrobe of the governor, shuffled past. This was all his baggage.

In the afternoon the official friend was informed that His Excellency of Lè was anxious to pay his respects, and four o'clock was fixed on as the hour of interview.

I cannot say that any very great preparations were made on our part for the great man's reception. A rude *charpay*, or native bedstead, was the official friend's throne of state; the cedar-grove his hall of audience; a faded dressing-gown, thrown over a flannel shirt of dubious hue, his robe of ceremony; his crown, the grey forage-cap of the Simla Volunteers; and his courtiers some three or four sunburnt Englishmen in their shirt sleeves, with beards of a month's growth, and the appearance generally of Californian gold-diggers, while all were remarkable for that winning and conciliating demeanour towards foreigners that the Briton is so famous for, especially when those foreigners are, as we courteously term them—niggers!

But the Sikh swell was wonderfully "got up." A small but beautifully folded turban, of a delicate pink, framed his frank, animated, intelligent countenance. The rest of his dress was of a snowy white, save a handsome "cummerband" or girdle, of Kashmir fabric. A jewelled baldric passing over his right shoulder, supported his sword; and his moustache and beard were short and trim, though the former was curled upwards, giving that *air troupier* to the face which the Sikhs so much affect.

He sat down on a railway-rug at the "official friend's" feet, and then motioned to his followers to set down the "nuzzer," or gift of ceremony, which consisted of sweetmeats, baskets of apricots and apples, of sugar-candy, of sheep, of a brick of tea, and lastly, of a timid little antelope, all which he prayed the "official friend" to accept.

The interview was not a long one; and, after our illustrious visitor's departure, we delighted our coolies and disgusted our servants—who looked on them as their peculiar perquisites—by instituting a grand scramble among the former for the sweetmeats, the apples, and the apricots.

And a glorious scramble it was—young and old, men and women, joined in it—pell mell! topsy turvey on the grass!

The ladies had by far the best of it. Whether it was that they were fonder of sweets, and therefore more eager to get them, or that their garments afforded greater facilities for pocketing, or that the men were chivalrous enough to let them snatch more than their fair share, I know not, but when the shower of fruit had ceased, and all squatted down to feast on the spoils, those of the women seemed inexhaustible. In the midst of them—the life and soul of the merry party—sat a lady in a yellow hood, and clad in a ragged robe of the same colour; she was a nun, and strange to say, the only one we saw while in Ladâk, though these Lamahs of the feminine gender are said to be nearly as numerous as their monastic brethren.

She had been the leader of the Amazons throughout the fight; ever in the thick of the *mêlée,* where the rain of fruit fell fastest, there her yellow garments were conspicuous amid the moving mass of drab jackets, of turquoise-studded lappets, and striped petticoats. And now, when the feasting was nearly over, and her companions were trying to adjust their somewhat tousled attire, ever and anon would she dive into some unexplored corner of the yellow robe, and produce therefrom more, and yet more apricots, not tempting to the eye indeed, for they were bruised, and broken, and mashed into pulp; but to judge from the gusto with which they were devoured, very pleasant to the taste.

These nuns are a calumniated race. More than one writer has poked indifferent fun at them—attempted mild facetiousness at their expense. To judge from the personal appearance of these ladies, it was clear that they had all taken the veil for the simple reason that they were tired of singing—

> "Nobody coming to marry me,
> Nobody coming to woo;"

being so hopelessly plain that even in that country of coarse visages, suitors held aloof! &c. Now, I beg leave most emphatically to protest against such a conclusion. This was the only nun we saw, and she, though not exactly a Venus, was undoubtedly the best-looking woman we saw in Ladâk, always excepting the little grass-shoemaker who sat by the wayside weaving sandals at Kyelang. Here is her profile; judge for yourselves.

She was a most jovial *religieuse;* but I wonder

what my Lady Abbess would have said, could she have seen the holy maid's frolics—"her nods, and becks, and wreathed smiles."

THE NUN.

We left our grove of cedars early next morning, and marched for about eight or nine miles, to a large village on the right bank of the Indus, called Nurla. The road wound round the steep and crumbling sides of a series of ravines, and was very narrow in some places, hardly affording a safe footing. The abode of a hermit was pointed out to us, perched like an eagle's nest on a rock many hundred feet above us. This saintly personage had been there many years, and spent his whole time in mental abstraction, prayer, and contemplation of "the ten thousand virtues of Boodha." He hoped by a perseverance in this course of training to arrive at last at perfection; meanwhile, the devout in the neighbourhood regularly supplied him with food.

Nurla is one of the largest, most populous, and thriving villages that we saw; it is lower and warmer than the country we had passed through as yet, and the fruit-trees and plantations of willow and poplar grew very abundantly. Here we breakfasted and changed coolies. From Nurla to Khallach the road followed the course of the Indus, which is here shut in on either side by lofty cliffs of red clay; every now and then these recede from the river's bank, leaving a slip of land, generally under cultivation. Shortly before reaching Khallach the road crosses a deep watercourse, and then ascends a steep pitch, on the top of which is a large clear tank, fed by a little aqueduct from the hill above it, whose waters find an exit on its south side, and help to make green the fields of the Khallach villages; its cool depths promised joys unspeakable to dusty wayfarers; and without more ado,

regardless of publicity, of the fact that they stood on the king's highway, three shameless pale-faces stripped, and plunged them in the tank.

Our camp was pitched about a quarter of a mile on, just below the village, which is considerably above the level of the river.

A swim in the tank, before starting, braced our limbs for the toils of the day. Shortly after leaving Khallach we crossed the Indus by a good wooden bridge, which the Sikhs have fortified on the Lè side of the stream. One or two fierce-looking warriors of that nation were lounging about, whose duty it was to collect the bridge-toll from all passers. After this we left the Indus valley, and turned up to the left, entering a narrow gorge, along which the path wound for some miles, continually crossing and recrossing the stream which flowed through it towards the Indus. A sudden and steep ascent up the cliff on the right, for about one thousand feet, brought us on to a large bed of yellow clay; after crossing which, the picturesque village and monastery of Lama Yurru came in sight.

The Lamahs account for this strange deposit of clay by the fact that it once upon a time formed the basin of a large lake. Their traditions say that the founder of the Lama Yurru monastery, a Lhassan priest, named Narossa, cut through the rock a channel for the waters of the lake, which falling into the ravine up which we had marched, soon left bare the clayey bed on which the sheet of water once had lain.

We camped below the village, which was built at a great height above us, and was itself overtopped by the towers and flags of the monastery.

Next day we crossed the Photo La Pass (thirteen thousand feet), after an easy and gradual ascent of about three miles, and shortly after halted for breakfast, on the banks of a little stream, which came rushing out of a narrow defile across our path; a frowning precipice rose on each side the rivulet, and on the summit of the right hand one was the village of Henasko.

We pitched our camp a few miles further on, near the dilapidated village of Kerboo. The

SCENE ON THE MARCH BETWEEN KERBOO AND SURGOL.

river here widened out into a broad but shallow stream; the meadows along its bank were marshy, and abounded in wild fowl, principally teal, which afforded us a good afternoon's sport. Next day we crossed the Pass of Namikar, and halted at a place called Turgot, situate in a green valley, shut in by lofty and barren mountains. Shortly before camping we had passed an enormous figure, sculptured in rude *alto relievo* on the face of an isolated rock that towered high above the pathway; the figure was that of Chamba, a Thibetan divinity, and its proportions were colossal; it seemed to mark the limit of the realms of Boodha—to say to Mahommedanism, "Thus

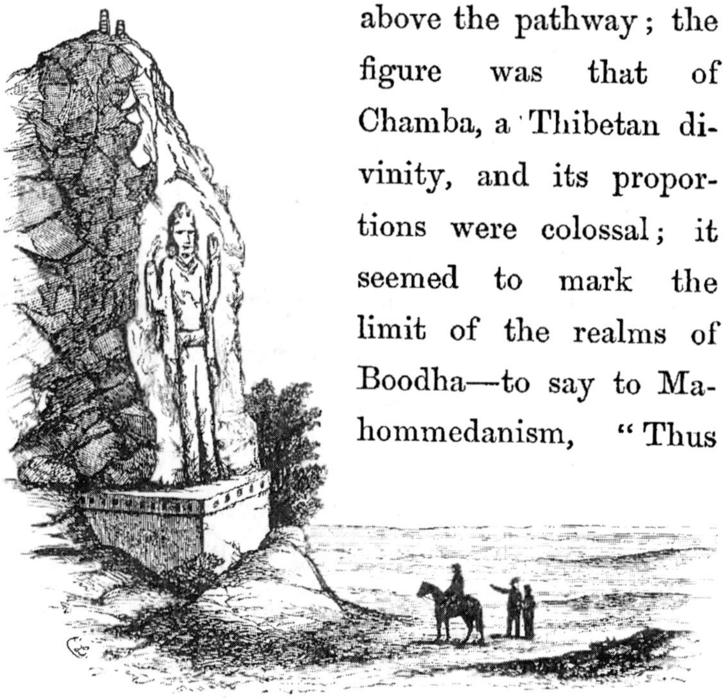

FIGURE OF CHAMBA.

far, and no farther;" and will, doubtless, stand sentry here long after the fierce tide of the religion of Islam has swept past it.

After this we saw no Lamaseries, Tchoktens, or Manis; reached villages where, in defiance of the laws of Boodha, poultry were reared, and killed, and eaten; and now, much to the satisfaction of Ali Bux and the delight of the travellers, eggs, plain boiled, or poached, or beaten up into savoury omelets, again smoked upon the board.

There is no doubt but that Mahommedanism is spreading rapidly in those districts of Ladâk and Balti which border on Kashmir, and is changing the habits and character of the inhabitants; doing good, inasmuch as it prohibits "chang" and checks intoxication; doing harm, inasmuch as it brings with it Kashmirian dissoluteness, mendacity, and fraud. Whether its effects are beneficial or otherwise is, therefore, a question which I must decline answering; for, influenced as I am by reminiscences of the fat capons and savoury omelets of Mahommed, I am not prepared to judge impartially between him and Boodha, especially when I bethink me what atrocious beer the latter brews.

A march of about eleven miles through a long narrow valley brought us to Paskyun, which is a large but ill-built, and widely scattered hamlet, and its inhabitants are all Mahommedans. We remarked that Ali Bux here adopted a voluminous green turban, which he wore throughout the rest of the trip; and now that he had reached a country of true believers, of brother-followers of the Prophet, comported himself generally with a dignity and lofty arrogance of demeanour quite edifying to behold.

After breakfast we left the valley of Paskyun, and ascended the heights to the left. The summit reached, we found ourselves on a broad plateau, on whose stony surface not a blade of grass was visible; it sloped down gradually in front of us, narrowing as the slope became steeper, and finally came to an end where the waters of the Turu river, coming from the south-west, meet with those of the stream, the Wakachu, we had followed as far as Paskyun.

The view from the crest of this plateau, looking to the left up the course of the Turu river, was one of the most striking I ever saw. I attempted to sketch it, but my brush has failed to give any idea of its grandeur. The Turu river, which at its confluence with the Wakachu spreads out to a great breadth, is crossed by a series of small wooden bridges and causeways, and on the tongue of land between the two rivers is a Sikh fort, built on the same principle as that of Lè. After crossing the river, we encamped on its left bank opposite to the fort.

We followed the left bank of the Turu next day till it was joined by the Dràs river, a mountain stream of considerable size, up the left bank of which our path led us for many a weary mile of up and down hill. Towards evening we reached a substantial wooden bridge, and soon after we encamped at Thusgam, on the right bank of the river.

This was a long and trying march, especially for four-footed beasts and their riders; the path was in many places so narrow that ponies could with difficulty find a footing, and the white bones of many an ill-fated animal that had slipped and fallen over caught the eye as it glanced below—a sight unpleasantly suggestive of what your own fate would be were your steed to make a false step: the pedestrians of the party had much the best of it.

Our poor little antelope, the gift of the Governor of Lè, died to-day of fatigue, Noura said, to whose charge it had been confided; but over-eating was probably the real cause; we had killed it with kindness. Misfortunes never come singly; one of my milch goats, too, departed this life during the day's march, and with her, alas! her infant son, who had seen the light of day only a few hours.

The poor foolish little lady had shown no signs of an intention to increase and multiply before leaving Simla; but ere we reached Lè her interesting but most inconvenient condition had attracted my notice, and I strongly recommended the goatherd to leave her behind at the capital of Ladâk. But, no! Melibœus was obstinate;

he felt convinced that the happy event would not take place before we reached Kashmir, where, urged he, the mother would be sure to obtain the best medical advice, and our halt would be long enough to enable the offspring to gather sufficient strength to bear the fatigue of our onward journey.

His arguments were so plausible that I permitted myself to be overruled, and madame marched out of Lè so cheerily and with so light a step, considering the weight she carried, that all my apprehensions of a premature *accouchement* vanished.

But

> "mutabile semper
> Fœmina."

Ladies never know their own minds, even in cases such as this, when we naturally feel inclined to place some little reliance on their powers of calculation. Poor Melibœus!

> "En, ipse capellas
> Protenus æger ago; hanc etiam vix, Tityre duco."

Such his plight some days after. The catastrophe had, however, not yet taken place; she had the sense to wait till the end of the march, and at Kurgyl, at 6.30, p.m., exactly, a fine kid came into the world. At 6, a.m., the next morning, mother and child were doing well. Mamma had nibbled a mouthful or two of fresh grass, and was as well as could be expected; and baby, bless its little heart! had already exhibited no contemptible powers of suction! "Pack 'em in a khilta, sahib, and order a coolie to carry 'em," suggested Melibœus. No sooner said than done; wrapped in a warm blanket and pillowed on soft hay, they were made as comfortable as circumstances would admit of; but the *khilta* proved their last resting-place—it was a dead weight that the coolie bore when he marched into camp.

A shower of rain fell that night, and in the morning the mountains around us were white with fresh fallen snow; but the valley was green and clothed with luxuriant vegetation. As we advanced and came in sight of the hamlet of Dràs, the valley opened out into a little plain, which now widening, now narrowing, stretched for miles before us. We halted at Drás, and pushed on next day eagerly, for in front of us, behind the blue lines of mountains topped by snowy peaks, lay our Promised Land — the "terrestrial paradise," Kashmir. Our road led us along a succession of green valleys opening into each other by narrow defiles; there were no trees as yet, but the ground was covered with a thick carpet of long grass, shrubs, and flowers. We camped that night close to a glacier which filled up a deep ravine in the mountain-side to our left. This monstrous icicle, seen in the glare of day with its thousand streamlets trickling out from under the cool shadow of the opaque mass, was a pleasant neighbour enough; but when evening came on, and the grateful plash and murmur of each tiny rivulet ceased one by one as the frost shut them up for the night with his icy chain, and all around was dark, and motionless, and cold, we wished him farther; and with the first streak of dawn were up and away far from his frigid vicinity.

After a walk of a few miles, the valley suddenly ceased, and our path dived headlong into a deep chasm, o'er which

> "The crags closed round with black and jagged arms;"

the descent was almost precipitous, but happily not a long one; at the bottom was a mass of ice and hardened snow, in which were embedded rocks, stones, and gravel; through this a small stream with difficulty worked its way, and a few yards further on leaped into the black void of an abyss beyond. We could not see where it lighted after its spring; but the sound of a continuous splash rose up from the depths below. A difficult zigzag cut in the face of the rock led us up the opposite side of the chasm. A forest of stunted birch-trees clothed its summit, through which the path wound on, gradually ascending to where, about half a mile ahead, was the ridge of the pass. This ridge reached, Kashmir was before us!!

It is a thing not easily to be forgotten, that first glimpse of Kashmir. The softer beauties of the vale proper, indeed, are hid from you. It is one of the many valleys whose sides, stretching from the snows of the Himalaya to the warmth and fertility at their base, seem to bind together summer and winter with one mighty wreath of green forest, that lies before you; and it is in these valleys, which form as it were the "woods and forests" of the immense domain of which the *vale, par excellence,* is the flower-garden—that, to my mind, Kashmir's richest and rarest gems, as far as inanimate beauty goes, are to be found.

The descent of the pass into the valley was very steep and rugged; thick forest began as soon as the ridge was passed, and our path led through—

> "One vast mass
> Of mingling shade, whose brown magnificence
> A narrow vale embosoms."

The name of this valley is Sindh, so called from the river which flows down it, and the pass we had just crossed was the Seogi-Lá, a continuation of the same range which we had before scaled by the Bara Lachi Pass. This chain of hills forms a natural boundary between India and Thibet.*

We halted for breakfast at the foot of the pass, and tempted by the unaccustomed beauties which surrounded us, lingered so long, that at last we decided on camping there for the night.

In the afternoon the Major and I, hearing that unmistakeable marks of bears had been seen in the vicinity, plunged into the jungle in different directions. Our expedition resulted in our stalking each other with great skill. After walking for about two hours, I distinctly heard in the jungle on my right the crashing and snapping of dried sticks and small twigs, and the rustling of the larger boughs that bent before the weight of some large animal. He was coming straight towards me; and crouching down in the dense underwood, with finger on trigger, I anxiously waited for the appearance of the mass of black fur I felt so sure of. But the sounds suddenly ceased. I crept cau-

* *Vide* Cunningham's *Ladâk.*

tiously towards the spot whence they had seemed to come; I stopped and listened; the rustling had again commenced; he was quite close now; I was safe to get him; and in another moment I saw!—the ruddy face of the gallant Major peering at me out of the thick cover, with an odd expression of blank wonder, of disappointment not unmingled with disgust; though the mouth smiled a smile which tried to be jolly, and the voice in a tone which tried to be hearty, said—"By Jove! I thought you were a bear!"

We pushed on for the next two days at the rate of twenty miles a day, following the course of the Sindh river through a lovely country; it was one continued descent, but so slight as to be hardly perceptible, save here and there, where the glen narrowed so much as scarce to give the stream a wide enough channel, and it and our road jostled each other for right of way. I cannot compliment the Maharajah on his highways.

We met a number of soldiers *en route*, bound for Lè, the garrison of which they were to relieve; they straggled for miles along the road without an attempt at formation, and each individual warrior appeared to have laid down separate "Dress Regulations," to suit his own particular fancy.

Our moonshee was a different man now that he had reached the happy valley, his whiskers resumed their sleek appearance and curled proudly upwards; he discarded the unsightly wraps that had disguised his figure during the march; a tight pair of cherry-coloured over-alls encased his slender limbs, and he rode at our head with a jaunty swagger, "witching the world with noble horsemanship!" We christened him C——n on the spot!

Throughout the second day's march, our path led through a continuous orchard of walnut, apple, and pear trees growing wild, mingled with sycamore, horse-chestnut, and ash; after awhile, houses built of logs appeared, and here and there land had been reclaimed from the forest and put under cultivation; towards the close of day we crossed the Sindh river by a good wooden bridge, and ascending the left bank, which rose to a considerable height above the river, came in sight of the famous Vale of Kashmir, bathed in the warm rays of the setting sun; in the far distance rose the snowy peaks of the Pir Punjal, tinted with the rosy light of eve, and between stretched a vast expanse of undulating plain, which bore on its broad bosom cities, lakes, and gardens; but even as we looked the sun sank behind the western range of hills; and though the snow-crowned brows of the distant hills still sparkled in the gleam of his parting ray, over the valley shadows gathered fast, and veiled it from our sight.

It was dark ere our tents were pitched, and the night was far spent ere all our coolies arrived; but the trusty Ali Bux was no such laggard, and our dinner was ready ere the "official friend" had made his appearance. On his arrival a bevy of civil and military authorities came to greet him with offerings of fruit and sweetmeats; we forgave them their unseasonable intrusion for the sake of the dessert it afforded us—peaches, grapes, plums, pears, and apples! And so to bed, haunted by a vague suspicion that the natives, liars though they be generally, were pretty near the truth when they called Kashmir a "terrestrial Paradise," and that Tom Moore was not far wrong when he sang—

> "And oh ! if there be an Elysium on earth,
> It is this ! it is this !"

CHAPTER XII.

"The wild Carmanian waste,
And o'er the aërial mountains which
pour down
Indus and Oxus from their icy caves,
In joy and exultation held his way,
Till, in the Vale of Cachemire, far within
Its loneliest dell, where odorous plants
entwine
Beneath the hollow rocks a natural
bower,
Beside a sparkling rivulet he stretched
His languid limbs."

WE were now about twelve miles from Sreenuggur, and had the choice of accomplishing that distance either by land or water, for we had reached the chain of lake and river that stretches throughout the valley, and forms the principal means of communication from point to point. We chose the former mode of progression, much to the annoyance of the moonshee, who would evidently have preferred the "cushioned ease" of the latter, and at about 9, a.m., found ourselves some three miles on our way, lying in the shade of a magnificent chunar-tree, devouring the accumulated results of a six weeks' dearth of news; for a "dâk" runner, with three English mails, had that instant met us.

The chunar-tree (*Platanus orientalis*) is a very striking object in a Kashmir landscape; notwithstanding their extreme luxuriance of foliage, and the stately height to which they attain, they are said not to be indigenous to the valley, but to have been introduced by a governor of the name of Ali Mirahan Khan, who held office from 1642 to 1657, under the Mogul dynasty. Of the mosques and garden palaces, the marble founts, and sculptured pillars, with which a succession of Mogul emperors embellished the valley they loved so well, but few remain intact, and even these show marks of neglect, dilapidation, and rapid decay; but the chunars are in the lusty prime of life—more lasting memorials of the magnificence of the Delhi emperors than all the costlier monuments, the work of men's hands.

The suburbs of Sreenuggur call up reminiscences of those of Constantinople, with their turbaned tombs of departed Moslems—their green luxuriance of nature, and squalid penury of art—but the fancied resemblance grows less and less as you approach the city. To enter it you pass no imperial walls or massive gateways, but little by little the houses huddle themselves closer together, and at last form a street, narrow and dirty and stony enough to induce a relapse into your dreamy memories of Stamboul, while here and there a high-featured face and stately form, in ample turban and flowing robe, stalks by and helps to keep up the delusion. But now a gap in the wall of houses on your right lets in a stream of warm light on the dark, foul footway, and through it you see close by you, not the broad bosom of the breezy Bosphorus or the crowded waters of the Golden Horn, but a sluggish stream, glittering in the sunlight, and covered with boats of all sizes; some, heavily laden barges, are being slowly punted up stream, while others of lighter build glide past merrily, propelled by the rapid strokes of half-a-dozen paddles—it is a busy scene. And on the opposite side the river you see reproduced as in a mirror a *facsimile* of the bank you stand on—the same houses, the same landing-places, the same people —for it is the Jhelum that you look on; and on his right bank and on his left stand the crowded dwellings of the capital of Kashmir—Sreenuggur.

We are here stopped by a crowd of boatmen, women, and children, who assure us that it is the proper thing to dismount, and take boat for the rest of the journey; we are nothing loth, for the sun is hot, the lanes of the city close and odoriferous, and the broad pathway of the Jhelum is decidedly preferable. We step into the nearest boat, and are soon lying under an awning of rough matting, leisurely proceeding up-stream, paddled by one old woman, two men, a boy, who does more work than the other three put together,

SREENUGGUR—BRIDGE OVER THE JHELUM.

and a child of tender years, who brandishes a mimic paddle, which retards rather than aids our progress.

We peep out from under our awning to the right and to the left on a strange scene. The houses on either side stand close to the water's edge, and some, supported by piles, project over it; every here and there a flight of steps leads down to the river, looking up which you see a vista of picturesque lanes opening out into streets beyond—foul, dark, and odoriferous as the one you have just escaped from. And as a foreground to the picture, sitting on the steps nearest the water, are groups of straw-coloured women, with handsome features, and soft black eyes, clad in long wrappers of maroon-coloured stuff, and engaged in the wholesome occupation of washing themselves, the somewhat arduous one of washing their children, and the pleasant and congenial one of talking scandal. While round and about you bubble up on the surface of the stream the little black heads and merry faces of urchins who, though they scarce can walk, can swim, and dive, and desport them in the water like so many water-kelpies.

And so on, 'neath the shade of bridges, whose wooden piers for years four hundred have striven, and still strive, to goad that patient stream into fretfulness, but in vain—his current flows on calm and placid as ever, unmindful of the interruption their passive resistance causes. He will soon have enough knocking about after Baramoola* is passed; besides, he loves Kashmir,

* "From Barâhmula to Mozafarabad, the Behat (Jhelum)

and reluctant to leave her motherly embrace, dawdles on with lingering step; but once away from her influence, he dashes on, a raving torrent, "lamenting," say the Kashmirians, "in foam and clamour, his departure from their beautiful valley;" soon houses disappear, and in their place green banks, planted with rows of poplar-trees, cast their cool shadow on the water; and here and there a strange little edifice meets the eye, in front of which, lounging in easy-chairs, are the sort of people you see on Ryde pier, rather more hairy, possibly, and *degagé* in their attire; but smoking, and reading the *Times* and *Bell's Life*, discussing in the same language the self-same topics, and staring at you with the self-same air of impertinent curiosity, which says as plainly

pursues an easterly course for 100 miles. The total fall between these places is 3800 feet, or 30 feet per mile, and the character of the river entirely changes from a placid and sluggish stream to a raving torrent. Below Tattamula, and about sixteen miles from Barâhmula, the rocky cliffs rise almost perpendicularly from the river to a height of 300 or 400 feet; and in some places that I noticed, the bare steep cliffs were not less than 800 feet above the stream."—Cunningham's *Ladâk*, p. 114.

as if the words were spoken—"And pray, who the deuce are you?"

A few more strokes of the paddles, and we are moored under the left bank of the river, and mounting the steps of a landing-place, find ourselves on a tolerably broad pathway shaded by the poplars before-mentioned; on this pathway, and overlooking the river, is a long row of small, square, two-storied houses, built of wood—exaggerated sentry-boxes, in fact, each with its private flight of stairs leading down to the water's edge.

These "bungalows" (as, with an oriental disregard for truth, it is the fashion to term them,) have been built by the Maharajah of Kashmir, expressly for the accommodation of British visitors; and although neither spacious nor well-furnished, their rooms are a pleasant change enough from the confined dimensions of a diminutive tent. The one opposite which we had landed had been reserved for the "official friend," and in front of it we found him and the rest of our *camarades de voyage* seated in arm-chairs, ostensibly receiving and replying to the complimentary addresses of a gorgeous assemblage of Sreenuggur swells—the mayor and corporation of the city-but in reality vying with each other in the luscious labour of emptying the baskets of grapes and peaches presented by those worthies, the fruit of whose gardens was evidently more acceptable to the travellers than the flowers of their speech.

To the back of these bungalows stretches a grassy plain, where tents are pitched and horses picketed; and in their front rolls the smooth waters of the Jhelum, here about two hundred yards in breadth. Its opposite bank is planted with poplars and other trees, and every here and there the white canvas of an Englishman's tent peeps through the green foliage; while up and down to the right and to the left stretches the "Visitors' Reach," as this part of the river is called. The scene is not a strikingly beautiful one, but it is fresh and green, and home-like, reminding one of the boating and bathing of one's youth—of Jerseys, sculling matches, and four-oars!!

Three of our party decide on taking up their quarters in the house the Maharajah had provided for us, but the others say they prefer "dwelling in tents,"—a difference of taste which is most opportune, for the visitors' bungalows are not calculated to hold more than three people at the outside.

One of the first personages who meets you on your arrival in Kashmir is the "Baboo," a functionary whose duty it is to see that all visitors to the valley are made as comfortable as possible. He is your landlord, your upholsterer, the director of your post-office arrangements, your general agent—in fine, a most useful fellow; and one of the first things he does is to show you a book, in which are inscribed all the fashionable arrivals of the season. Half-an-hour's talk with him (he speaks capital English, and is very civil and obliging) makes you *au fait* of all the doings of the little colony of British visitors; he is a sort of peripatetic *Court Journal* and *Morning Post* all in one.

Of these visitors, you will find that some are mighty hunters, and are ever away in the wilds, only showing their bronzed faces in Sreenuggur once or twice a month, when they return for more powder and shot, or a peep at the home papers. Others pursue sport, too, but in a milder form, and may be seen from early morn to "dewy eve" plying the fisher's gentle art on lake and river; others sketch; and others in a desultory way affect natural philosophy, and pretend to make collections of flowers or stones, accordingly as their tastes happen to be botanical or geological; while others, and by far the greater number, do *nothing*, and do that nothing very well!

With the one exception of the photographer, who was indefatigable, we all at once enrolled ourselves in the ranks of the listless band of "do-nothings," and provided ourselves at once with a boat a-piece—an indispensable article of equipment in *that* volunteer corps—to procure which requires no effort, save the mental one of choice; for immediately on arrival a swarm of boatmen buzz around you, pressing on your perusal certificates of industry, or the reverse—of good conduct, or a general aptitude for rascality (which, by the bye, is with them the best recommendation) from former employers.

It is not an expensive addition to your establishment; you pay your boatmen five shillings a month a-piece, and they supply the boat, moor it at your door, and are always ready to paddle you up or down stream, whither you will; night or day they are at your service; nor are their avocations strictly confined to lake or river, they will act in any capacity, and can turn their hands to anything; could they keep them from picking and stealing, they would be invaluable servants—but their honesty, alas! is not above suspicion;

> "De boatman dance,
> De boatman sing,
> De boatman him up to ebery ting;"

and notwithstanding his want of discrimination between *meum* and *tuum*, the coxswain of a boat generally succeeds in gaining the entire confidence of his master for the time being.

The boats are long, narrow, and flat-bottomed, built like canoes, and at the extremities slightly curved up out of the water; the boatmen sit and paddle at either end, while the centre of the skiff is reserved for the "Sahib." Here he reclines on cushions, shaded from the sun by an awning of matting, and thus lounging, is by no means an object of pity.

We fell quite naturally into "the even tenor" of the ways of the "do-nothings;" and as the shadows began to lengthen on the first day of our arrival, we found ourselves stepping into our canoes and preparing for our evening pull on the still waters of the Jhelum as if we had done so all our lives.

The river, from the "Visitors' Reach" to the last of the bridges—and there are seven—forms the Mall or promenade—the Rotten-row of Sreenuggur. This is the invariable resort of the "do-nothing" in the cool of the evening; languidly smoking a cigar, he leans back on his cushions, and is paddled up and down, and down and up again, till it grows dark, when he is paddled off, and is seen no more till the next evening—for the existence of the "do-nothing" is not a sociable one. We noticed them passing and repassing each other without the most distant sign of recognition; they do not attempt to extend the circle of their acquaintance, *that* would be doing something—a something, too, that would involve a still further labour, such as a morning call, or possibly an invitation to dinner; and exertions arduous as these are quite incompatible with the *dolce far niente* of a "do-nothing's" life.

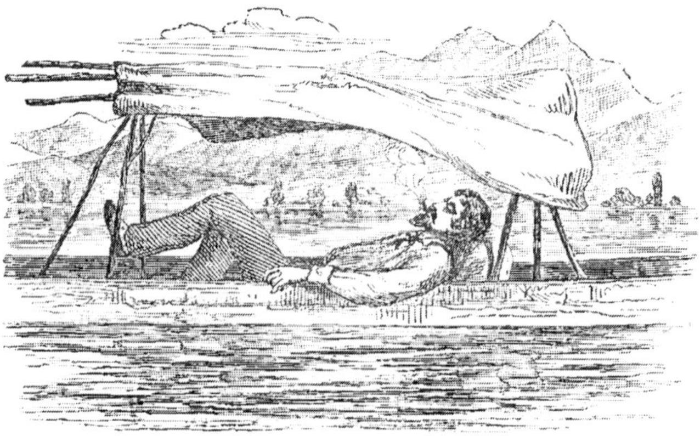

DOLCE FAR NIENTE.

Near the arches of every bridge are groups ot fishermen, standing erect in the bow of their boats, "throwing a fly" with most commendable perseverance. "That sahib," said one of my boatmen, "has been here for four years, fishing the whole of the season, and every morning and every evening has whipped the water under that very identical arch. Oh! it's a great sahib for fish!" Possibly the man lied, and no doubt he exaggerated greatly; but during the ten days we spent at Sreenuggur, I never passed that bridge, morning or evening, without finding that devoted disciple of Izaak Walton at his post, rod in hand, whipping the stream as perseveringly as ever.

The banks of the river present much the same appearance as they did in the morning, save that the bathing machines are fuller—for such we discovered some strange wooden erections to be, which, moored at intervals to the shore on either side the river, seem to float on the water. These were now in constant requisition, and we should have come away deeply impressed with the personal cleanliness of the inhabitants of Sreenuggur, had we not remarked that the dirty old loose wrapper—the usual dress of the Kashmiris of both sexes—was invariably donned again after the operation; a relapse into which "vile habit" must militate fatally against the healthful and cleansing results of a dip in the Jhelum.

But now the sun has sunk below the houses of the city to our left, and its slanting rays can no longer annoy you, so the boatmen stow away the awning, and permit your gaze to wander upwards from the bathing machines, boats, and landing-stairs to the trellised windows of the picturesque houses above you; some of which, perched on slender piles, lean over the water, and seem to have serious intentions of taking an evening stroll on stilts. Seen dimly through the delicately-carved woodwork of the half-open lattice, you will now and then, if you are lucky, catch a glimpse of the graceful form and face of some fair Kashmirian girl, with braided tresses, and dark bright eyes slyly peeping out on the crowded river below. And now, his day's work done, the pleasure-loving Kashmiri begins to enjoy himself; sounds of mirth and laughter, of music and merriment, are borne out to you from those mysterious casements, for there abide the queens of dance and song—

> "Those songs that ne'er so sweetly sound,
> As from a young Kashmirian's mouth,"

and boats freighted with bundles of dim drapery, whence peep little jewelled hands and slippered feet, glide past you—

> "Youth at the helm and pleasure at the prow."

The Rotten-row of Sreenuggur has, I regret to say, its "pretty horsebreakers" too!

But it is time to turn round, for we have reached the seventh bridge, and 'tis a long pull back far up "the dim, rich city," to our home under the poplar trees.

The delight of a plunge in the river is our first waking thought, and attired simply in dressing-gown and slippers, we shuffle, half-awake, into our boat, which is paddled into mid-stream. Then, after pausing for one timorous instant on the gunwale, we throw ourselves overboard, and float lazily down stream, exulting in the refreshing chill of the water, as yet untouched by the sun: then coffee or chocolate, a cigar, a stroll up the river-bank, a leisurely toilette, and so to breakfast about ten of the clock—such the daily programme of our early morning performances in Kashmir.

And now a crowd of Kashmiris, manufacturers of shawls, gunmakers, workers in leather, in papier maché, jewellers, tailors, shoemakers, watch-menders, &c. &c., besiege us. They are remarkable for mechanical talent. Kashmir shawls have achieved a world-wide reputation;

their gun, pistol, and matchlock barrels are much prized by natives, holding a second rank to those of Scinde only. Of their papier maché, all those who have the luck to see the Exhibition of 1862 will have an opportunity of judging. The jewellers, shoemakers, and tailors only want a pattern; they will imitate it with the minutest accuracy; and if your watch is out of order, you may entrust it without compunction to that ill-looking fellow in a greasy gaberdine, who will squat down in a corner of your room or tent, deliberately take it to pieces, and perform all necessary repairs there in your presence.

We sent word to the two great shawl merchants of Sreenuggur that we would honour them with a visit, if they would fix the day, for the shawls that are hawked about by the natives who frequent "Visitors' Reach" are not worth an inspection.

It is a pleasant morning's lounge (though apt to prove an expensive one) through the show-rooms of the Kashmir shawl-merchants. Of these, Muktah Shah and Syf-oolah Baba are the most celebrated, the former for the shawls manufactured in a loom, the latter for those worked by hand; though the productions of the loom are much the most valued of the two kinds of manufactures, I had the bad taste to prefer the others.

They are most comfortable fellows, and own the best houses in the city, these merchant princes of Kashmir. After landing at the little wharf which stretches out into the water from beneath the shade of their well-built warehouses, you are shown through a narrow door, up a narrow staircase, and soon find yourself in a light, airy, well-carpetted room overhanging the river; a small table and a few chairs in honour of European visitors, a low divan for the accommodation of Orientals, form the sole furniture of the apartment. The master of the house soon makes his appearance. He is a tall, high-featured, well-looking Mahommedan, with a partially shaven upper lip, but long and glossy beard; his manners are those of a past age—past, at least, for Europe. He is an Oriental Sir Charles Grandison.

After a little preliminary converse, during which tea, grapes, and biscuits are brought in and laid out on the little table before you, the topic "shawls," by utter chance, as it seems to you, comes on the *tapis*, and then slaves, barefooted and obsequious, come staggering in under mighty bales, whose contents are soon spread before you—treasures of the loom and cunning hand. Sir Charles Grandison now seats himself —I will not say *squats*—at your feet, and as each marvel of art is in succession displayed, courteously points out to you its beauties, discusses its merits and probable value; in fact, he begins to bargain, though the word fails to convey any notion of his manner. He is not a linen-draper trying to show off his goods to the best advantage, but rather a country squire showing to his guests with a pardonable pride his stable, his pigs, his fatted bulls of Bashan, or whatever else may be his hobby!

The shawl dealers complained one and all of the slackness of trade. The demand for Kashmir shawls has dwindled in extent proportionably as British supremacy has spread northwards from Bengal Proper; for we are content with—in fact, rather prefer—tweeds and broadcloths, sombre suits of dittos, to the gorgeous colours of the Kashmir fabric; Ellwood's patent helmets, or the modest wide-awake, to the graceful folds of an embroidered turban; and are wont, either by elastic braces, or often simply by the nearer propinquity of button and button-hole, to support our nether garments, making the costly "cummerbund," or girdle, an *objet de luxe* quite uncalled-for; and even our ladies, much as they prize a real Kashmir shawl, are apt to think that one hundred pounds can be spent much more profitably than in the purchase of one; whereas in olden days, the native Courts were an unfailing annual source of revenue to the Sreenuggur manufacturer. The fall of Lucknow had been his last and bitterest blow!

Having spent a morning or two with Messieurs Muktah Shah and Syf-oolah Baba, and paddled two or three times up and down the river, you may be said to have *done* Sreenuggur, for there is but little else to interest the traveller in the city itself.

There are indeed one or two musjids or mosques of great antiquity, and not without some claim to architectural beauty, but in order to get to them I should have to lead you through back slums so noisome, that I will, out of a due regard for your comfort, content me with assuring you that they are not worth seeing. There are in odd corners remains of walls built of great slabs of stone, mute witnesses to a past magnificence, which offer a strange contrast to the ricketty dwellings of half-burnt bricks and wood of which they frequently form the foundation, and on which the antiquarian would love to ponder, and the sentimental traveller to moralize, but I lack both the lore of the one and the sentiment of the other, so will hold my peace.

There is the Hurree-purwat Fort, overhanging the town, which, seen from the river, is a striking structure enough, but it will not bear inspection; its walls are weak, indebted to plaster mainly for the imposing effect they produce at a distance, and its *three* cannon are honeycombed. There is the palace of the Maharajah, a long labyrinth of brick walls and dingy woodwork skirting the Jhelum's left bank, here and there relieved by a gilt dome, mounted on a whitewashed tower; it

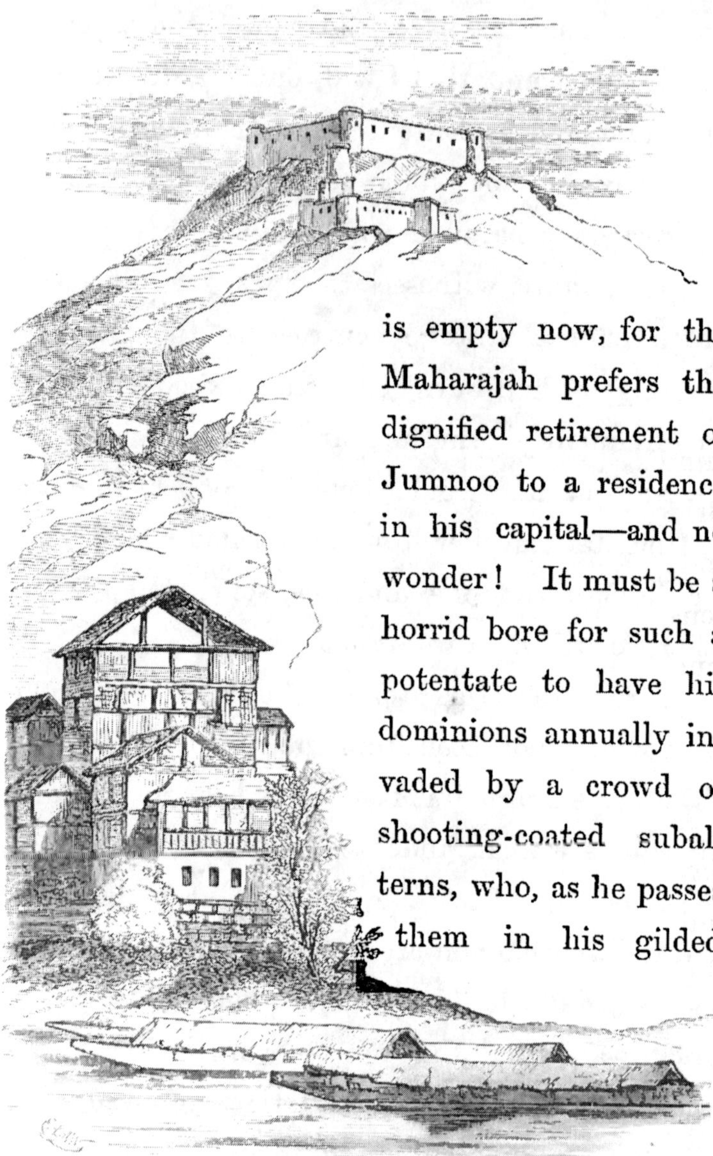

is empty now, for the Maharajah prefers the dignified retirement of Jumnoo to a residence in his capital—and no wonder! It must be a horrid bore for such a potentate to have his dominions annually invaded by a crowd of shooting-coated subalterns, who, as he passes them in his gilded

HURREE-PURWAT FORT.

barge, vouchsafe to acknowledge his presence by a condescending nod or a patronizing wave of the hand, notwithstanding that these Goths and Vandals put indirectly so many Company's rupees into his Highness's pocket.

The bridges, too, are picturesque, built entirely of wood, resting on piers formed of massive blocks of cedar (deodar), and some have rows of shops on them, flanking the footway on either side, reminding one of ancient prints of Old London Bridge; but all these sights have been sketched and written about by able pencils and learned pens, and you, reader, doubtless know quite as much about them as I do—for

"Who has not heard of the vale of Cashmere"?

Let us, then, pass away from the crowded pathway of the Jhelum, leave behind us Sreenuggur and its busy traffic, and tell our boatmen to explore that canal to the left, the greensward and overhanging foliage of whose thickly-planted banks promise a pleasant change to the tumble-down houses and dark lanes that have so long hemmed us in.

It leads—

> "Through the mountainous portal that opes
> Sublime, from that valley of bliss to the world,"

to the "Dal," or lake, behind the city.

To speak truly, it requires a great amount of imagination to recognise Tom Moore's "mountainous portal" (of which Feramorz leads us to form such extravagant notions) when you see it. A pair of massive wooden folding gates, through which your boat glides, is all that at first meets the eye; and they actually and *prosaically* form the entrance to the lake. But away to the right, a considerable eminence, known as the Tukht-i-Soliman,* or Solomon's Seat, rises from a green

* "The legends of the country assert that Solomon visited this valley, and finding it covered, except the hill on which some Mahommedan has dedicated a temple to King Solomon, with a noxious water which had no outlet, he opened a passage in the mountains (at Baramoula), and gave to Kashmire its beautiful plains."—Forster.

On legends such as these a supposition that the Kashmiris are descendants of the Jews has been built—a supposition which is borne out by the personal appearance of the race—their garb, the cast of their countenances, and the form of the beards. There is a belief, too, that Moses died in the capital of Kashmire, and that he is buried near it.

The Suliman, or Sulayman, however, of Oriental legend,

HENASKO.

bed of gardens and orchards, and *may* be said,

must not be always supposed to be identical with the son of David.

"No name is more famous in the East than Solomon; he succeeded his father David, according to their belief, when only twelve years old, at which age Omnipotence placed under his obedience not only mankind, but even the elements and the genii, good and bad. His throne was magnificent beyond idea — 12,000 seats of gold being placed on the right for the patriarchs and prophets, and 12,000 on the left for men learned in every science. The birds were his constant attendants, screening him like a canopy from the inclemencies of the weather; whilst the zephyrs, wafting him wherever he wished to go, rendered horses or any carriage unnecessary. All the wonderful traditions, however, relative to Solomon, are not confined to the son of David. The heroic or fabulous ages of the Persians go far beyond those of the Europeans—the world, agreeably to their system, being peopled thousands of years before Adam by ethereal or igneal beings, governed by a succession of seventy-two Solomons.

"The supernatural powers supposed to be vested in these ante-Adamite monarchs, as well as in the King of Judah, are figured to have been chiefly derived from the curious talismans they were said to have possessed—to which allusion is often made, not only in their poems and romances, but in their graver works, and the Koran itself; such as the 'Seal,' the 'flaming sword,' the 'impenetrable cuirass,' the 'shield' of Solomon—which last, they add, was bequeathed by Jān biu Jān, one of the ante-Adamite kings, to the father of mankind, who carried it to Sarandib (Ceylon), where it was many ages afterwards discovered by Kayumars, the first king of Persia, from whom, descending to his grandson,

*poetically** speaking, to "form one side of a grand portal to the lake." But for the other side you

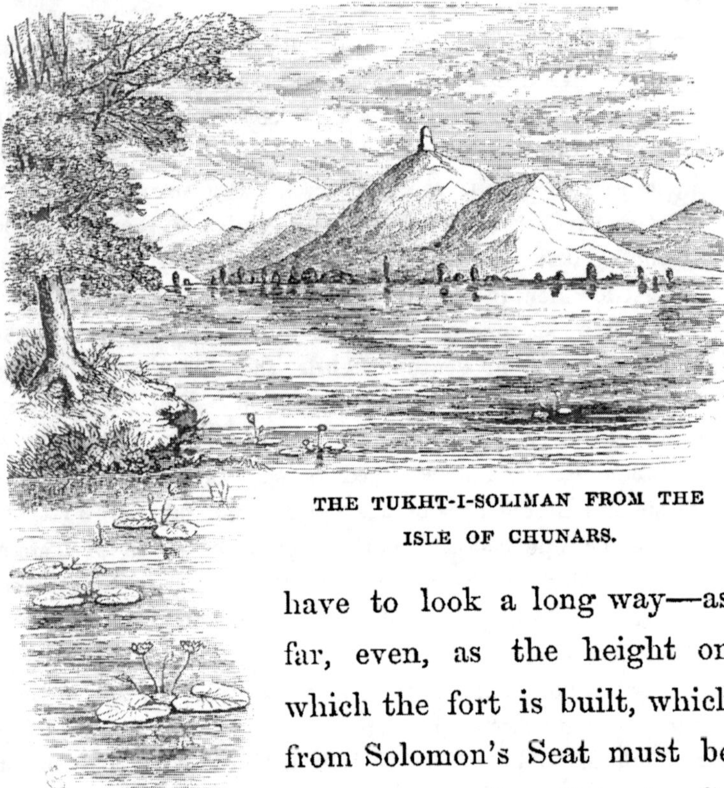

THE TUKHT-I-SOLIMAN FROM THE ISLE OF CHUNARS.

have to look a long way—as far, even, as the height on which the fort is built, which from Solomon's Seat must be some three miles distant. So that this poetical portal is, to say the least, a tolerably wide one!

Tahmuras, it was by that prince employed so successfully in his war with the Dīves, that he got the surname of Dīv-band, or chainer of demons."—Vide Richardson's *Dictionary*.

* Forster says so in sober prose.—Author.

But we have still a long pull through a narrow channel ere the broad expanse of lake opens out in front of us; and then its surface is so thickly covered with the broad leaves and rosy flowers of the lotus, and the tangled green of the sinhara, or water-nut—its sides so concealed by floating gardens*—that it is difficult to form any idea of

* "Another and an important use made of the abundant water-surface of Kashmir, is the formation of floating gardens. Various aquatic plants spring from the bottom of the lakes—as water-lilies, confervæ, sedges, reeds, &c.; and as the boats which traverse these waters take generally the shortest lines they can pursue to the place of their destination, the lakes are in some parts cut as it were in avenues amongst the plants, which in shallows are separated by beds of sedges and of reeds. In the latter places the neighbouring farmer attempts to establish his cucumber and melon floats, by cutting off the roots of the aquatic plants just mentioned, about two feet under the water, so that they completely lose all connexion with the bottom of the lake, but retain their former situation in respect to each other. When thus detached from the soil they are pressed into somewhat closer contact, and formed into beds of about two yards in breadth, and of an indifferent length. The heads of the sedges, reeds, and other plants of the float are now cut off and laid on its surface, and covered with a thin coat of mud, which, at first intercepted in its descent, gradually sinks into the mass of matted roots. The bed floats, but is kept in its place by a stake of willow driven through it at each end, which admits of its rising or falling in accommo-

its size. The first glimpse is, however, enough to convince you of its beauty.

To the left, the eye wanders lingeringly over a fertile tract of lake and meadow, to where the

dation to the rise or fall of the water. By means of a long pole thrust among the weeds at the bottom of the lake from the side of a boat, and turned round several times in the same direction, a quantity of confervæ and of other plants is torn off from the bottom, and carried in the boat to the platform, where the weeds are twisted into conical mounds about two feet in diameter at their base, and of the same height, terminating at the top in a hollow, which is filled with fresh soft mud drawn from the bottom of the lake, to which sometimes wood ashes are added, though much more frequently omitted. The farmer has in preparation a large number of cucumber and melon plants which have been raised under mats, and of these, when they have four leaves, he places three plants in the basin of every cone or mound, of which a double row runs along the edge of every bed, at about two feet distance from each other.

"No further care is necessary, except that of collecting the fruit, and the expense of preparing the platforms and cones is confined to that of the labour, which altogether is trifling, as the work is very soon done.

"Perhaps a more economical method of raising cucumbers cannot be devised, and though the narrow beds are ordinarily almost in contact by their sides, yet by their flexible nature they are so separable that a small boat may be readily pushed between the lines without injuring their structure, and for the most part they will bear a man's weight, but generally the fruit is plucked off from the boat."—Moorcroft's *Travels.*

VIEW, LOOKING UP THE SURU RIVER.

Hurree-purwat Fort shows a castellated line against the blue sky. Then, ranging the horizon from left to right, you see successively the Nusseem Bagh, or the Garden of the Morning Breeze; behind which rises in the distance a blue line of hills, which come nearer and nearer as the eye travels on to the right, till they seem to spring from the very banks of the lake, just where a thick grove of trees marks the site of the "magnificent Shahlimar;" and in a line between it and you is the little Isle of Chunars, called by the Kashmiris the Chandee-ke-Cank, or Silver Island. To the right of Shahlimar, again, are the Gardens of Pleasaunce, the Nishat Bagh; and from thence the gaze rests on a lovely prospect of hills mirroring themselves in the smooth surface of the lake they encircle—wherever the lotus will allow them an uninterrupted view of themselves, past the little "Golden Island," or Sonar-ke-Cank, the Peri Mahal, or Fairy Castle—a picturesque ruin overhanging the water; back to the Tukht-i-Soliman, beyond which again rise the snowy peaks that tower above the passes out of Kashmir.

Let us tell our boatmen to paddle slowly on to the isle of Chunar, which seems to float on the water about a mile a-head of us. It is just big enough to afford a resting-place to a little ruin

THE ISLE OF CHUNAR.

so dilapidated that the eye fails to trace its original form ; and to two lofty chunar trees, which completely overshadow it, and hide with pious care its venerable remains from the rude gaze of the passer-by.

The day is now drawing to a close, and we see the lake at its best—

> "At sunset, when warm o'er the lake,
> Its splendour at parting a summer eve throws,
> Like a bride full of blushes, when lingering to take
> A last look at her mirror at night when she goes."

The boatmen are quite alive to the beauty of the scene—though so common a one to them—for they love and are proud of their far-famed lake; gathering lotus-flowers as they paddle homewards, they wreathe them round their turbans, and sing long ballads in praise of the loveliness of their valley and the charms of its fair daughters, beating time to their voices with the pleasant plash of the paddle.

There is one little drawback to the enjoyment of boating on the lake, which, strange to say, Tom Moore omitted to mention; neither Feramorz, nor Lalla Rookh, nor even Fadladeen, say or sing one word about it—and that is, the mosquitoes, which are as monstrous in size as they are pertinacious in their attacks. They are always in season, too; wild duck migrate, and the lotus ceases to bloom, but the mosquito of Kashmir appears to be quite above all such frailties—he never moults, or loses his appetite—

> " Fee-fo-fum,
> I smell the blood of an Englishman,"

he hisses in your ear, and woe to the Saxon he takes a fancy to.

I have purposely omitted to describe the Shahlimar Gardens whilst recounting the beauties of the lake in the sunshine. It, like Melrose, to be "viewed aright," should be visited "by the pale moonlight."

> "For the gay beams of lightsome day,
> Gild, but to flout, its ruins grey."

This queen of gardens does not look well by daylight; but at night, if properly bedecked with torches, and crowned with lamps, you do not remark the ravages Time has made in her complexion, and she still has power to charm—

> "Where the waterfalls gleam like a quick fall of stars,
> And the nightingale's hymn from the isle of Chunars,
> Is broken by laughs and light echoes of feet."

The proper thing to do is to give orders for a nautch at Shahlimar—to tell your Ali Bux that you will dine in the largest of the summer palaces—to read nothing but *Lalla Rookh* all day, and towards evening to step into your boat and glide over the still lake to the gardens, doing your best to feel

> "As felt the magnificent son of Ackbar."

It is by no means a difficult illusion to get up;

the accessories to the picture are all perfect—the smooth, rapid motion—the still, slumbering expanse of water, that wakes and ripples into a momentary smile as you pass, and then sinks back into its wonted repose—the sparkling, diamond-like drops that the quick strokes of the paddle dash up on to the broad lotus leaves, that quiver there an instant, and are gone—the mysterious rustle of yielding leaves as your boat presses through them in her course—the delicate-hued flowers that bend towards you in courteous welcome as your keel grazes their floating roots—the laughter which strikes on your ear as you pass rapidly by boats freighted with fair members of the *corps de ballet*—the blaze of torches as you land, which makes the sequestered bowers of the garden seem yet darker and more mysterious—the constant plash of fountains, sparkling in the light of the lamps that illumine them—and, better than all (for it is no phantom form, no shadowy spirit of air), the face that peeps playfully from under the white folds of a half-raised veil, fair enough to be that of Nourmahal, the Light of the Harem's self. With "aids to reflection" such as these, it is not difficult to imagine yourself for the nonce a "proud lord of the East."

Bernier, who visited Kashmir in 1668, thus describes the garden of those days:—

"The most beautiful of all these gardens is one belonging to the King, called Shalimar. The entrance from the lake is through a spacious canal, bordered with green turf, and running between two rows of poplars. Its length is about five hundred paces, and it leads to a large summer-house placed in the middle of the garden. A second canal, still finer than the first, then conducts you to another summer-house at the end of the garden. This canal is paved with large freestone, and its sloping sides are covered with the same. In the middle is a long row of *jets d'eau*, or waterworks, fifteen paces asunder; besides which there are here and there large circular basins or reservoirs, out of which arise other *jets d'eau*, formed into a variety of shapes and figures.

"The summer-houses are placed in the midst of the canal, consequently surrounded by water, and between the two rows of large poplars planted on either side. They are built in the form of a dome, and encircled by a gallery, into which four doors open; two looking up or down the canal, and two leading to bridges which connect the building with both banks. The houses consist of a large room in the centre, and of four smaller apartments, one at each corner. The whole of the interior is painted and gilt; and on the walls of all the chambers are inscribed certain sentences, written in splendid Persian characters. The four doors are extremely valuable, being composed of rare and large stone, and supported by two beautiful pillars. The doors and pillars were found in some of the pagan temples demolished by Shah Jehan, and it is impossible to estimate their value. I cannot describe the nature of the stone; but it is far superior to porphyry, or any species of marble."

It has now lost much of its beauty from neglect. Gaudy Hindoo paintings have here and there disfigured the walls and roofs of the summer-houses. Nor has the pencil or burnt stick of Brown, Jones, and Robinson been idle in portraying its familiar fancies on stucco and marble. But the "pale moonlight" softens down, where it does not actually conceal, these barbarisms of modern date. The porphyry pillars and galleried summer-houses are all there still; and the giant boughs of the graceful chunar trees (mere shrubs when Bernier saw them) now o'ershadow in their turn the formal poplars, and lend a charm to the scene it never knew in those old days—fully compensating for the results of Hindoo neglect and bad taste, and the unsightliness of British frescoes.

The streams that fed the canal, and which flow down from the mountains at the back, are now all turned off for purposes of irrigation, and the canal is dry and choked with weeds; the waterworks are waterless, save on gala nights such as this, when at the bidding of Englishmen the mountain streams resume their ancient channel, and seek the well-known path to Shahlimar, there to be tortured into waterfalls and *jets d'eau,* to be forced into pipes and 'prisoned in freestone reservoirs, while the fields and meadows languish for want of their fertilizing moisture. But I am forgetting; such a sentiment as that last was utterly unworthy of a son of Ackbar: and this reminds me that it would be as well to lay aside our assumed character for the present. It is dinner time! and chicken, cutlets, and sherry, porter and roast mutton, anchovy toast, and brandy and soda water, are dainties which poor Selim, though he seems to have liked his glass of wine, never dreamed of.

We dine in a spacious hall, open on one side to a mimic lake, bristling with water-spouts, and fed by a prettily-managed waterfall, whose stream falls over niches in which little lamps are gleaming, now brightly, now dimly, as the watery veil that covers them varies in its volume. On the other side a handsome corridor leads out on to a stone platform of some extent, whence a long vista of lamps and sparkling *jets d'eau* stretches away down to the large lake. This path of light tapers away till the eye loses it in the distance; the black shadows of the trees and tangled thickets of the garden close it in on either side, and above, in a sea of fleecy vapour, floats serenely the lady moon. On this platform preparations are being made for the *nautch.* Already has a white floorcloth been spread, the orchestra is beginning to tune up, and the merry prattle of women's voices tells us that the fair *artistes* are only awaiting our good pleasure to commence their performance.

Apart from the strange beauty of the scene around, the *nautch* itself was a vastly superior performance to any I had yet seen. The orchestra, of pipes and tabors, guitars and drums, occupied the back of the stage; in front of them sat demurely about a dozen nautch girls; and between the ladies and our arm-chairs stretched the white floorcloth on which they were to dance. While on either side was a closely-packed row of turbaned heads, among which we easily recognise our friend Syf-oolah-Baba; and torch-bearers and boatmen, mingled with our own servants, are grouped at the back.

The musicians remained seated—a great improvement on the habits of their class down country, who move backwards and forwards, as the dancers advance or recede, singing louder than the prima donna herself; here, however, they contented themselves with playing a low, soft accompaniment to the girls' voices; and their venerable beards, finely-cut features, and picturesque dress, formed a pleasing and appropriate background to the picture.

The *ballet* commenced at a sign from the Jemadar, or master of the revels, a little wiry, bright-eyed old man, who seemed to rule the *corps de ballet* with a rod of iron. Obedient to his nod, two of the nautch girls rose, the orchestra played a wild prelude, and then began a somewhat monotonous pantomime of waving arms and supple forms, in which (a strange contrast to our notions of dancing) the feet bore the smallest part. The two *danseuses* moved slowly and smoothly towards, and round, and away from each other, never allowing the feet to leave the floor; accompanying their gestures, which are certainly graceful and expressive, with a low, plaintive chant, that at intervals broke forth into a wild burst of song, whose harshness grated on *our* ears, but was received with unequivocal signs of approbation by the *native* audience.

Jacquemont says—"Leur danse est déjà, pour

moi, la plus gracieuse, et la plus séduisante du monde.

"Les entrechats et les pirouettes de l'opéra me semblent comme des gambades de sauvages de la mer du Sud, et le stupide trépignement des nègres ; au reste, c'est dans le nord de l'Industan que ces natch girls sont le plus célèbres." But I am not prepared to echo the learned Frenchman's sentiments.

Of the two first performers, one was a beautiful girl, tall and *svelte,* with a complexion fair as that of many of our own countrywomen ; the other showed at a disadvantage by her side, and appeared to have been selected purposely as a foil by the proud beauty. Their costume, with the exception of their head-dress, a little fez-shaped cap of gold embroidery, from beneath which their dark hair fell in long plaits, was hideous ; clothed from chin to foot in a shapeless shroud of stiff brocade and amber-coloured satin, which effectually concealed any grace of form they might possess, their attire was about as complete a contrast as is well possible to the *maillots et jupes de gaze* of our *figurantes.* Imagine a Quakeress doomed to array herself in such colours, it is thus she would arrange them.

The rest of the performance was but a repetition of the first act—the same monotony of dance and song, varied only by a change of performers—and we begin to yawn, and wonder what o'clock it is, which the Jemadar perceiving, orders the tall beauty and her dusky companion again to the front, places long wands in their hands, and as the band strikes up a livelier air the Amazons enact a mimic combat.

This over, we seriously think of going, but insist, before we actually depart, on one more song from "Ghoolābie," the *belle* of the evening; but she is coy, and has got a cold, and is tired; in fact, she wants pressing, and it is some time ere she can be prevailed on to lay aside her Dehli looking-glass, the gift of some one of her many admirers, and yield to our entreaties. At last she comes forward and sings, after an affected little cough or two, some such words as these:—

"Sleep! sleep! let me sing thee to sleep.
Sleep while my tresses o'er thee
Fall in a fragrant caress.

Sleep, for to watch thee reposing
Is to me deep happiness.
Sleep, sleep, let me sing thee to sleep.

"Wake! wake! let me kiss thee awake.
Wake from thy dreams of beauty
To the warmth of a real embrace.
Wake from the chain of night's shadowy thrall.
Wake! see the morn in my face!
Wake, wake, let me kiss thee awake.

"Stay! stay! let me pray thee to stay.
That the red light of returning day!
Nay! 'tis not sunset yet!
'Tis but the gleam of his evening ray,
That slants through the lattice still.
Stay, stay, let me pray thee to stay!"

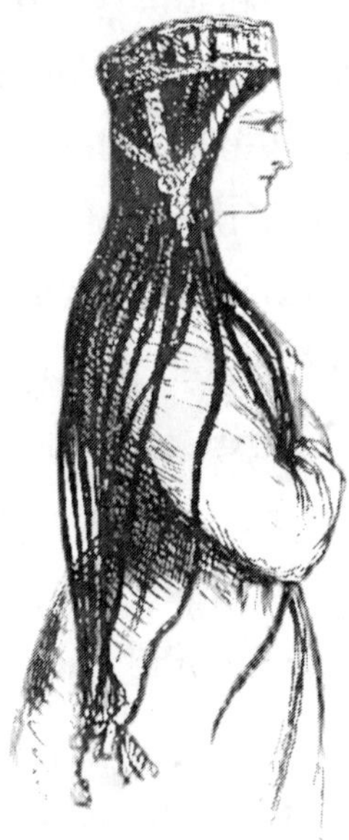

GHOOLABIE.

But the last stanza fails to *stay* us, and there is now a general move, for the lamps begin to burn dimly, and the *jets d'eau* to give symptoms of a failure of the water supply; and betaking ourselves to our boats we paddle homewards o'er the still waters, while our boatmen enliven their toil by repeating snatches of the parting song of the fair—

"Kashmirian's *ἱπποδαμοιο*,"

which still rings in their ears.

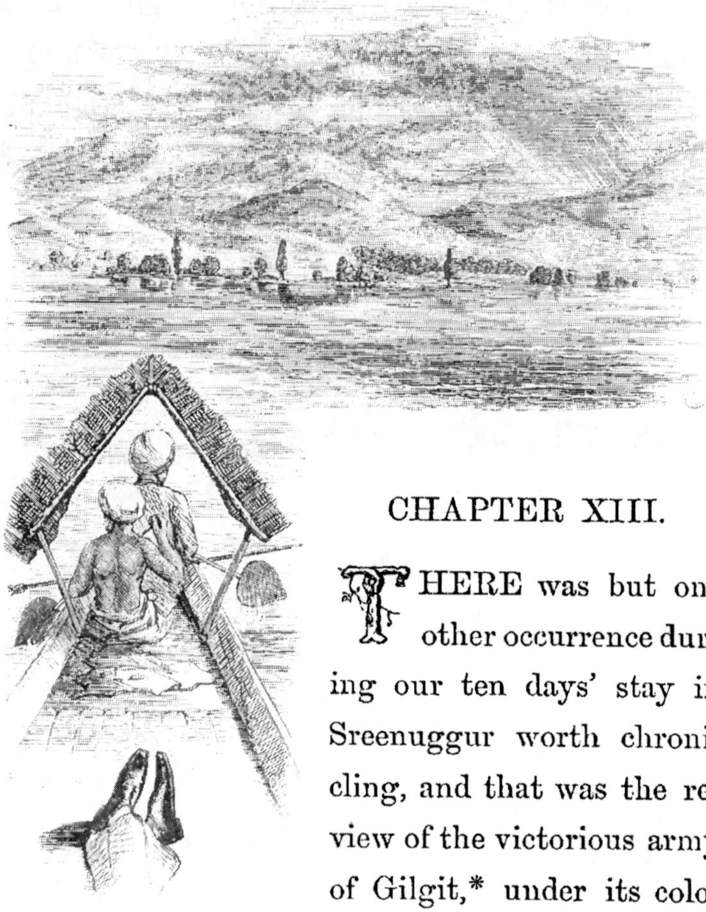

CHAPTER XIII.

THERE was but one other occurrence during our ten days' stay in Sreenuggur worth chronicling, and that was the review of the victorious army of Gilgit,* under its colonels, Devi Singh and Dooloo Singh.

This occurred one Sunday afternoon just outside the city. The army consisted of three regiments of foot, the two other branches of the ser-

* Vide Appendix.

vice did not put in an appearance; the horses of the cavalry, we found, had all been sent out to grass, and as for the artillery, we could get no satisfactory replies to our inquiries about it; in fact, some of the sceptically inclined amongst us presumed to form doubts as to whether it really existed.

They marched past in slow time steadily enough, except when they kicked their shoes off in their strenuous exertions to "throw the foot out well." This occurred frequently, and the sight of a man in the front rank suddenly stopping, backing on to his rear-rank man and shoving him out of his place, staring wildly about for a second or two till he caught sight of the missing article of equipment—his shoe—lying in the dust, pouncing on it, and picking it up just in time to save its being trampled on by the next advancing company, and then doubling back into the ranks again, was one calculated in a measure to detract from the martial effect of a manœuvre, however well it might have otherwise been executed.

After marching past they went through a few

light infantry movements, and to our dismay fired off at the spectators an immense amount of blank ammunition, fortunately without any serious result, and the review was over.

The uniform of the Maharajah's troops was a strange mixture of the old British regulation coatee and the Oriental turban, and their equipment somewhat similar to that of our own soldiers in the days of flint-locks, save that they all wore at their side a sharp-edged "tulwar" in its wooden scabbard.

Colonel Devi Singh, who was introduced to us, was one of the handsomest men I ever saw in my life, and looked the soldier all over; his turban, small, but beautifully folded, was tastefully arranged; his coatee of red cloth blazed with gold embroidery, and fitted him well; white trousers, and shoes of Oriental shape, completed his costume.

His colleague in arms was a strange Hudibrastic figure that Hogarth would have rejoiced in; the grotesque effect of his personal defects (he was not an Antinous) was heightened by the bad taste and incongruities of his dress, and

Colonel Devi Singh was, I thought, rather ashamed of him, although quite conscious that his own appearance gained by the contrast.

DEVI SINGH AND DOOLOO SINGH.

We left Sreenuggur on the morning of the 15th of September; our party now reduced to three, for the photographer had discovered an old chum amongst the visitors to the valley, who had prevailed on him to desert us, and the two Riflemen could not afford the time our somewhat circuitous route homewards needed.

The first part of our journey was by water; we had the option of going by land, but a ten days' sojourn in the Capua of Hindostan had served to eradicate much of our Himalaya be-

THE RIFLEMEN.

gotten energy, and soften our muscles. It was delightful to watch the smile of contentment on our moonshee's face when we told him to order boats for our journey up stream to Islamabad.

We now discarded the boats in which we had lounged about the environs of the city, and hired in their place large barges big enough to carry self, bed, baggage, and servants—of these we had one a-piece; the moonshee and his men another; and Ali Bux, with his pots and pans, "khitmutghars," and the rest of the servants, followed in two more. It was quite a little fleet, and our Ladakhi coolies, relieved of their loads, marched up the river bank beside us. Our progress was slow, for we were towed up the stream by drag ropes, harnessed to two or three men; but for people not in a hurry, and blessed with a climate such as that of Kashmir, it was the perfection of lazy travelling. It is seldom that it falls to one's lot to enjoy such perfect repose, such freedom from care, as on board one of these barges; one's sensations are precisely those, I imagine, of an infant in his cradle rocked by a kind but determined mamma; so long as you let her rock the cradle or pull the tow rope, as the case may be, and are content with the narrow precincts of your temporary abode, you are in all other matters the monarch of all you survey. If you want conversation you can hail a friend's craft, for we keep close together; if solitude, you can be deaf to his talk, should he be garrulously inclined, and read, write, draw, or sleep at your ease, for the boat is steady as a rock, and hardly a sound disturbs the completeness of the quiet around.

These barges are similarly arranged to the

boats we hired to explore Sreenuggur in; the centre, with all its breadth of beam shaded by an awning, is reserved for the traveller, and fore and aft are the boatmen or boatwomen, as the case may be. My crew consisted of sailors of the latter sex, and the privacy of my cabin was often invaded by an urchin, who was always clambering over the partition and otherwise misbehaving himself, thereby at times seriously disturbing my repose and exciting my wrath; but mamma always begged him off so ably, that the little rascal more than once received "backsheesh" for his intrusion. She was so handsome—a gipsy face, perfect in its outline, but weather-beaten, and deeply marked by constant exposure—young, indeed, in years, but already a matron in appearance; her complexion gave the strongest proof of the fairness of the Kashmirees, inasmuch as it was *freckled* by the sun, and her cheek glowed with the "imbrowning of the fruit," contrasting with the white of the brow which her long black hair had shaded.

And now let me employ this hour of ease in telling my readers a few matters of which I shall not have an opportunity of speaking when once marching begins again. I have as yet said nothing about the climate of Kashmir, but little of its inhabitants, and not one word about its government. I am bent on boring you, reader, but give fair warning of my intentions; so skip the next few pages if you will.

The valley of Kashmir is about 5000 feet above the level of the sea, but the climate is not so cool as might be expected at such an altitude. In September, the weather is what English people would call relaxing,—like a Devonshire summer; and in June and July it is at times, I am told, very hot; but wood, and water, and the snowy peaks that gird the valley in, alike conspire to cheat the sojourner into the delusion that it is not so. There is a Persian proverb, a quaint paradox enough, but which expresses the same idea in terser language—

> "Gurmush năh gurm ast;
> Surdush năh surd ast."

> "Heat there is, but hot 'tis not;
> Cold there is, but cold 'tis not."

In the winter, the hills around are covered with

snow, and it lies in the valley itself in January and February. The shooting at this season must be unrivalled—bears, leopards, deer, &c., all find their mountain haunts too cold, and seek the comparative warmth of the valley, and as native shikarees told us, actually *mob the villagers.* This somewhat startling statement, though doubtless a grossly exaggerated one, has yet a fair basis of truth to rest on. The magnificently antlered "bara-singa," or "stag of twelve tyne," may be shot close to the habitations of men; and the smaller species—the antelope and musk-deer—are equally daring in their approach to the haunts of their natural enemy. As to bears they must literally *swarm,* for during the fruit season the black bear abounds in the valley itself; and when food becomes scarce, the high lands too cold, and he is joined by his brown brother of the mountains, their number must be formidable indeed; but though thus numerous, it does not follow that Bruin will help to fill the bag of the sportsman in winter, for at this time of year he retires from the world, and hybernates in complete seclusion. At this season, however, when Kashmir would be a paradise to the British sportsman, the valley is forbidden ground.

It seldom happens that official people in India, and here all are officials, either of the sword or pen, can get leave of absence in the winter months. Nor, indeed, would it often be applied for could it be obtained, for leave in winter would debar the possibility of leave to enjoy the bracing air of the "hills" in the heats of summer. But when the "stamp of the iron horse" resounds through the length and breadth of the land, when Calcutta and Mooltan are connected with Lahore by a line of rail, and facilities for rapid travel increase, as day by day they are increasing, we may reasonably expect that the British possessions in India will cease to be a *terra incognita* to the tourist; and that the lakes and rivers of Kashmir, and the mighty chain of mountain and valley from Darjeeling to Murree will be visited by adventurous sight-seers, much as Switzerland is now. Of these travellers, the pioneers will doubtless be sportsmen, and it is to be hoped that the pressure from without which their advent will cause, will have the effect of doing away with the absurd restrictions now laid down by the Maharajah of Jumnoo, on all the approaches to the valley save two or three, and also with the prohibition he has thought fit to put in force against the winter residence of Europeans in Kashmir.

The people of Kashmir are a much-abused race —dishonest and mendacious, vicious and untrustworthy, sullen and disobliging, thieves, extortioners, no word is too bad for them!—and, strange to say, this is the general opinion formed of them, not only by the English visitor to the valley, who is no doubt looked on by them as fair game, but by the natives of the surrounding countries, by their own rulers, and *by themselves.* Talk to a Kashmiri on the subject of his countrymen, he will speak of them with abhorrence, warn you against having aught to do with them, apparently forgetting that he too is of the race he would taboo. The Dogra Dewan abuses the Hindoo Pundit, and *vice versâ;* through all ranks of society extends this amiable feeling of mutual distrust.

What everyone says must be true, to a certain

extent, and I fear that in this sweeping condemnation of the Kashmir character there is a large leaven of truth, but it is unjust thus to condemn them, without endeavouring to account for this moral degradation of a race so admirable in its *physique*, inhabiting a country so blessed by nature with beauteous scenery, wondrous fertility, and a glorious climate.

There is a native proverb, far from complimentary to the inhabitants of the happy valley—

> "Agar kuht-ool-rijal ōōftad, az eshan oons kum geeree,
> Eki Afghān, doum Kumboh, seum badzat Kashmiri;"

which may be rendered—

> "Should fate decree a dearth of men,
> Then, friend of mine, beware ye
> Of Afghan—Kumbo, scoundrel too,
> But worst of all, do thou eschew
> That ill-bred knave Kashmiri!"

There is no doubt that they were originally of Brahmin origin; and prosperous must have been the people—wise, beneficent, and energetic the rulers—in those old days, if tradition and legend are to be believed, and the mighty monuments of a past grandeur, long anterior to the days when Mogul wealth and taste embellished the valley, are to be looked on as faithful witnesses; but to this golden age succeeded centuries of oppression.

Little is known of the past history of this people till the year 1315, when Sheems-ood-deen ascended the throne, and introduced Mahommedanism. In 1586, Ákbar, the Mogul emperor, conquered the country; in 1752 it was subjugated by the Afghan, Ahmed Shah, and in 1819 by the Sikhs. Each succeeding race of conquerors seems to have pulled the reins of despotic rule and unjust taxation tighter and tighter, till, in 1846, after the Sutlej campaign, Kashmir was, under our auspices, handed over to the tender mercies of Ghoolab Singh, "in consideration of a pecuniary equivalent," to be his in independent succession; and its sovereignty is now a "source of weakness rather than strength to the great government which sold five millions of men for so many bags of silver."*

Poor Kashmir! when, after so many vicissi-

* Vide *Calcutta Review, Punjab Reports*, 1859.

tudes of slavery to a foreign yoke, the hand of a powerful, just, and merciful Government acquired the territory by force of arms in fair fight, and it seemed that at last its condition was about to be ameliorated, its old ill-luck stuck by it still! That hand had an itching palm, and they were again sold into the hands of the Philistines. The last state of that country was worse than the first, for Ghoolab Singh went far beyond his predecessors in the gentle acts of undue taxation and extortion. *They* had taxed heavily, it is true, but *he* sucked the very life-blood of the people; *they* had laid violent hands on a large proportion of the fruits of the earth, the profits of the loom, and the work of men's hands, but he skinned the very flints to fill his coffers.

We must therefore not be too hard on the Kashmiri; his faults are those that oppression fosters, and his virtues, for he has some, are his industry, his religious toleration, his observance of family ties and obligations, while for qualities of head and hand he is second to no Eastern race. As artificers, the pale, slim, sneaking denizens of the crowded lanes of Sreenuggur will compete with any in the East; and the sturdy, broad-shouldered, large-limbed peasant is a pains-taking and successful husbandman.

Amongst the many changes of masters which Kashmir has undergone, one class of men appear not only to have retained the religion of their Brahmin forefathers, but also a high position among their fellows. I allude to the Kashmiri Pundits—men of lengthy pedigree, of wealth and influence, who, thanks to their superior education and fitness for business, were largely employed by their successive conquerors, placed in posts of trust, and seemingly exempted from the forcible conversion to the creed of Mahommed, which was universally imposed on their countrymen. "Believe or die," such the motto of the Moslem Society for Promoting the Knowledge of the Prophet.

No Englishman can leave Kashmir without a sigh of regret that a province so full of promise should ever have been allowed to slip through our fingers. It would now have owned us as its rulers for near upon twenty years, and we should have benefited by the acquisition as much as, I hope, the people would have been bettered by our rule.

What a station for troops! An army, if wanted, might be quartered here, and the valley, as it slopes upwards to the surrounding hills, would afford numberless sites for sanitaria of various temperatures and aspects.

The reign of the present Maharajah Rumbeer Singh, the son of the rapacious Ghoolab Singh, is marked by an evident wish to govern wisely; but he is still surrounded by advisers of the old *régime*, who use their influence "not wisely, but too well;" no doubt, however, great improvements have been effected. An intelligent native official at Sreenuggur told us, that whereas the father had been "greedy of pelf, and pelf alone," the son, though quite conscious of the advantages of a huge exchequer, was "hungry after organization" ("sherista-ki-bhooka").

There was one circumstance of frequent occurrence during our wanderings in Kashmir, which would seem to argue an independence of feeling on the part of the people, and a disregard for the "powers that be," strangely at variance with the demeanour of men ground down and oppressed, and groaning under a heavy yoke; and that was the difficulty we experienced, not only in procuring coolies to carry our baggage, but also in making them work when they at last appeared. Often were our loads left in the middle of the path during a march by these truculent rustics, who would be off and away through the jungle into the tangled shade of the forest, with so fleet a foot as to baffle pursuit, regardless of the pecuniary loss their flight occasioned to them, for there was of course no day's pay for the runaway.

It was not that our burdens were heavy, on the contrary; or that the men were weak and unable to carry weight,—they were stout fellows, of athletic build and muscular limbs, and for carrying a paltry burden for a few miles would receive a high rate of wages. Yet they often preferred toiling under it for half the distance, and then bolting without being paid, to undergoing a little more labour with a certainty of reward for it. Now, we travelled with an agent deputed by the Maharajah to attend to our interests, were guarded by his soldiers, and one of our number was a civil officer of distinction; we marched, therefore, as it were, under the shadow of that rod of iron of which we heard so much, but which, when put to the test, seemed powerless to enforce obedience.

With the exception of the Pundits before mentioned, the Kashmiris are all Mahommedans; and the difference of creed between them and their Dogra rulers does not serve to lessen the unpopularity of the dominant race. Rumbeer Singh is a strict Hindoo; his favourite wife is "serious," and her influence over her lord and master is increased by the fact that his only children—two sons—are by her. Kashmir is literally overrun by Hindoo faqueers, detested by the people they prey upon, but supported and encouraged by the Government, and their numbers are rapidly increasing. Their appearance is loathsome in the extreme, and they are generally to be seen stalking about, or basking in the sun, stark naked, their long hair matted with filth, and their bodies smeared with wood-ashes. This state of things accounts for the neglect and dilapidation visible in all the Mahommedan buildings in the country; while on every side Hindoo temples are being erected. Hindooism has invaded the Tuhkt-i-Suliman itself; and there, on the very site of a Mahommedan shrine, has it erected a place of worship.

The food of the Kashmiri consists mainly of rice and fish; and a recent order of the Maharajah, forbidding the people to catch fish or to use them as an article of consumption—an order which, if carried out in its integrity, would result in actual starvation to many thousands—is an instance of the height of folly to which a weak mind, awed by superstition and swayed by priestcraft, can attain.

When a man (Hindoo) dies his troubles begin; should he die insolvent, his soul transmigrates into the body of an ass, doomed to bear burdens and be kicked and buffeted through life; should he have been, when in human form, a miserly hunks, avaricious and niggardly, usurious and a dun, he becomes a misletoe-bough—a parasite that sucks the blood of the tree that gives it a branch whereon to fasten (for such is the misletoe in the Oriental train of thought—to him the misletoe suggests no reminiscences of wine and wassail, of merry Christmases and stolen kisses). Such the belief inculcated by the Pundits, who further profess to be able to divine into what animals, vegetables, &c., the soul of a deceased man *successively* passes.

Now Ghoolab Singh, instead of becoming a misletoe, as he richly deserved, was turned after death into a bee—so said the Pundits; a decree went forth in consequence throughout the length and breadth of the land, that bees were henceforth sacred and must not be destroyed (whether the eating of honey was also forbidden I am not prepared to say). But this bee, though endowed with the soul of the deceased monarch, lacked his wary shrewdness; for one hot summer's day, when buzzing languidly on the surface of a cool stream, he was snapped up by a hungry fish—poor insect Jonah! But the soul of Ghoolab could not die, and therefore now inhabited a scaly tenement. The Maharajah's papa was a fish!!!

The result of this vile priestly fabrication was

the prohibition of fish as food; for the pious son was fearful lest some irreverent Moslem hook, with sacrilegious bait, should lure this royal fish—

> "Great Ghoolab's self now turned to fish,
> Might haply form a dainty dish
> For fisher man or boy;"

a catastrophe that would sadly interfere with the future transmigrations of that restless spirit. Fancy the orthodox soul of a deceased Maharajah dwelling in the heretic body of a Mahommedan fisherman. What would become of the *Moslem's* soul? Would it object to the intrusion, or fraternize and amalgamate with the new comer? It is a difficult question, and one which I suppose puzzled the Pundits; so they decided on preventing the possibility of their having ever to answer it, and thenceforth it was not lawful to eat fish!

Our boatmen were wont to be most facetious on this subject.

The Kashmiris, rich and poor, are passionately fond of tea, which reaches them, as it does the Russians, by land transport from China direct. The "semavar," or Russian tea-urn, is a common article of house furniture; and when I questioned them about it, they acknowledged that its shape had been imitated from a Russian model brought by some travelling merchant years ago from the north. This "dodge" for keeping tea hot had evidently impressed them with a great respect for the Muscovite; and they may be said to imbibe with each cup of comfort a spice of Russian influence. Muscovite intrigue may lurk in the aroma of each domestic teapot; and methought the very hiss of the steaming "semavar" breathed a covert warning, prophetic of the future.

Another piece of furniture in common use, and one which our boatmen said was also an article of foreign introduction, was the "kangri"—a little earthen vessel encased in basket-work, and filled with live charcoal: this all who can afford it are in the habit of carrying about with them, for its warmth's sake, in the winter months, hooking it on to their persons under their long wrappers. This is a practice which, Moorcroft says, "invariably discolours and scars the skin, and not unfrequently occasions palsy."

The Italians have a precisely similar custom; and it is quite possible that it may have been introduced into Kashmir by one of those Jesuit priests who were the first European wanderers in these parts; or that, *vice versâ*, the Italian priest may have introduced the Kashmiri custom into Italy on his return.

Our boatmen were possessed of vague notions of a happy time, long, long ago, when the men were all brave, hardy, and warlike, the women all virtuous. "The Kashmiri," said they, "wore short clothes then, and had no 'kangri;' but now, weak and effeminate, he wears a long wrapper, like a woman, and crouches for warmth over an earthen pot."

But all this time we have been progressing slowly but surely up the sluggish stream. The sun has set, and the little fleet comes to anchor.

With the first glimmer of daylight we are in motion again; and when we awake, the place of our anchorage is far behind us. Early in the afternoon we reach a bridge similar to those of Sreenuggur; the sides of the river are thronged with boats, and the banks with people. We have reached Islamabad; and leaving our boats, walk to the town, situated about half a mile from the river. We pitch our tents in a small walled enclosure, planted with giant plane-trees, and through which flows a clear stream full of fish; over it are built summer-houses, humble imitations of those of Shahlimar—our "lines have fallen in pleasant places."

We purchase a few of the patchwork carpets, for the manufacture of which the town is famous; dine in one of the cool summer-houses; and so to bed, full of virtuous resolutions to start on our march betimes on the morrow.

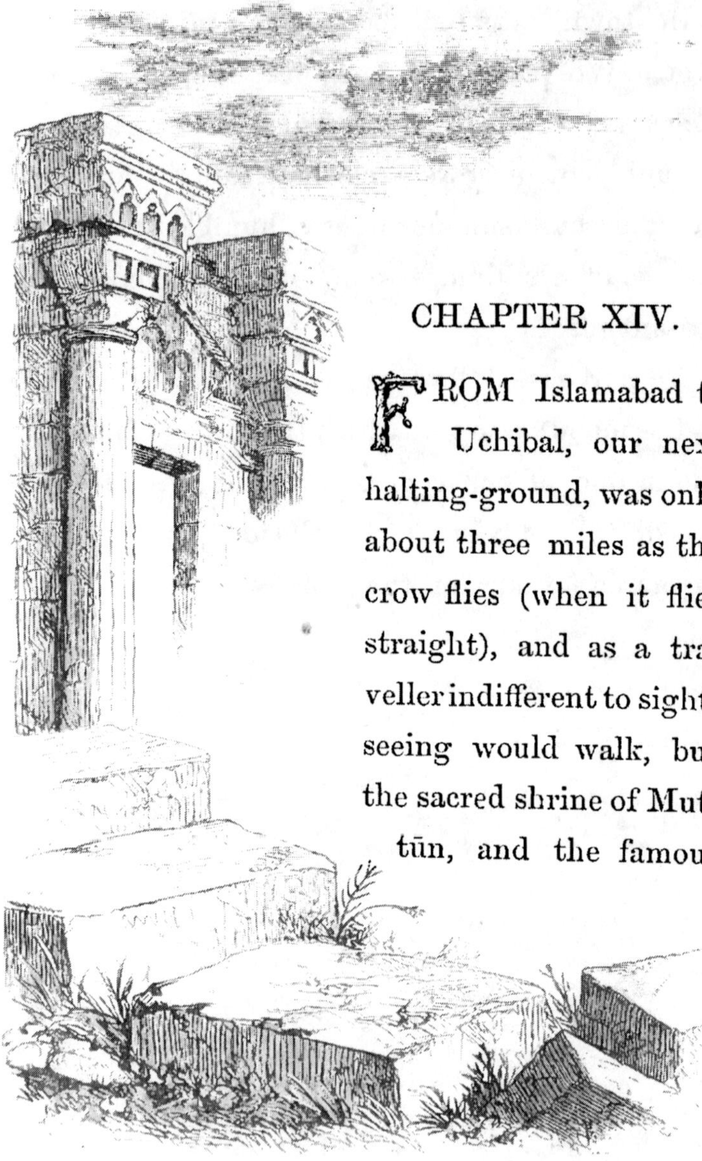

CHAPTER XIV.

FROM Islamabad to Uchibal, our next halting-ground, was only about three miles as the crow flies (when it flies straight), and as a traveller indifferent to sight-seeing would walk, but the sacred shrine of Mut-tūn, and the famous ruins of Martundh tempted us to make a *détour*, which turned our three miles into six or seven.

We breakfasted at Muttūn, just outside the holy precincts of the shrine, on the banks of a pleasant watercourse which flowed through the courtyard of the saintly building, and although its waters are continually employed in cleansing, not only from the spiritual stain of sin, but also from the more material mire of weary travel, a countless number of pilgrims, the little stream dances along merrily under the cool shade of the trees whose youth it helped to mature, and whose "green old age" it now still tends, with a sly little gurgling laugh, as though absolution was the best fun in the world, unsaddened by the weight of sin and sorrow it bears away, undimmed by the dust it washes off.

Our Hindoo servants were at once pounced upon by a crowd of hungry Brahmins, summoning them to "wash and be clean;" it was some time, however, before a bargain was struck. Our people wanted to do their cleansing cheap, to pay in a lump, to take a family ticket, as it were, for the performance; but this very praiseworthy and economical desire on their part was fiercely combated by the priests, whose threats and exhortations eventually gained the day. They made a very good thing out of our party, with the one exception of Nurput; to judge from the unfriendly, not to say stormy conclusion of his interview with the priests of Muttūn, I have every reason to fear that that big-fisted reprobate "bilked" his father confessor!

The temple itself is a small building of mean appearance, and the only point of interest it possesses for a European tourist is the reservoir in the centre of its little courtyard; this is almost as full of fish as it is of water. Imagine a barrel of red herrings, packed as herrings in a barrel usually are, with its well-salted contents suddenly brought to life again, all trying to get out of the barrel, and you can form a very tolerable idea of the fish at Muttūn—wriggling, shoving, clambering (a fact) on each other's backs, in their eagerness to snap up the morsels of parched grain we pitched in to them. This reservoir is fed by the little stream we have before mentioned, which finds an outlet over a sort of weir: down this it rushes with great rapidity, glad to leave so fishy a neighbourhood, and woe to the fat carp that incautiously allows himself to be drawn within the current's influence, flounder, flap, and struggle though he may, down he must go—down into the outer "world of waters;" cut off for ever from the cloistered cool of his shady tank, from the quiet society of his clerical associates, he'll have to work for his daily bread now, for no one will pitch him parched grain, or lumps of flour, unless indeed with a barbed hook in them, to aid his digestion; and oh, ye gods and little fishes! how his lay-brothers will bully the gorbellied old sinner when they catch him.

Here, too, was a "Visitors' Book," in charge of the Head Brahmin, containing the signatures of all the white excursionists who had found their way thither for years, mingled with those of dusky pilgrims of note. Among the former were those of many of our fair *compatriotes*, for annually is Kashmir the resort of an adventurous few, who sensibly prefer the delights of "roughing it" in pleasant company—the glories of its scenery, and its freedom from "crinoline"—to the gossip and morning calls, the effervescent scandal and flat gaieties of a Hill watering-place.

Our path led up a steep ascent for about three hundred yards on to a long, narrow plateau, which stretched out into the valley, and at the extremity of which were the ruins crowning the declivity, which sloped in a graceful sweep down to the level of the vale below.

RUINS OF MARTUNDH.

Though antiquaries assign to Martundh a date nearly as far back as the Christian era, its monolith pillars, massive walls, and imposing gateways still remain firm amongst the scattered *débris* that extend all along the plateau, showing that once upon a time a busy city stood there. Thanks to the enormous size and weight of the blocks and slabs of stone of which it is built, Martundh has resisted not only the slow march of time, the sudden shocks of earthquakes, but also the efforts made by man to sap its foundations; for so noble a monument of Hindoo greatness could not fail to be an eye-sore to the modern conquerors, who plied the pickaxe in vain, and found fire of no avail against its solid strength.

The people of the country attribute these ruins to the Pandus, the favourite princes of the heroic age of Hindoo history, whose exploits and wars with the rival family of the Kurus constitute the main subject of the great Sanskrit epic, the Mahabharata.

We lingered here till the sun was high in the heavens, and then strode down the slope across the valley to Uchibal, where we found our camp ready pitched. Uchibal was the scene of many an imperial merry-making in the good old days of Mogul rule, of Shah Jehan and Jehanguire: now the gardens are desolate and neglected, a tangled desert of weed and briar; but the stream, like a true philosopher, flows on calmly and contentedly as ever; his low murmurings utter no complaint, no regret for the pomps and vanities that are no more; they are rather, as it were, the gentle purring of a spirit at peace with itself, and inclined to be the same with all the world; welcoming the solitude of to-day as a pleasing contrast to the dust and noise, stir and bustle, and all the inconceivable nuisances of the imperial court of yesterday. It is a lovely spot, the luxur*iance* of an ever-present nature amply consoles

RUINS OF MARTUNDH.

the modern traveller for the want of the past luxur*iousness* of Oriental art.

We here provided ourselves with "shikarrees,"

or native trackers of game, and sending the moonshee with most of the tents and servants, and all the heavy baggage, by the direct road over the pass out of Kashmir, turned off to the left with a small "flying camp," intending to scale the wall of Nature's building that shuts in the valley by a different route, unfrequented by man, but of Bruin the brown, of the bear of the mountains a favourite haunt, at least so said the "shikarrees," and "*pucka*" Kashmiris though they were, they spoke truth.

Pucka. I have used it at last, that word of Hindostanee birth and Anglo-Indian adoption, the delight of the old inhabitants, but the horror of new arrivals from home, who watch with very natural dismay the encroachments the tongue of the black has made on the tongue of the white, and who shudder at the enormous percentage of Hindostanee with which the Indian residents interlard their speech. It is bad taste, they say; so thoroughly Indian; and they are right. They, however, little know how easily the habit is acquired; and some few months after, you will hear these very people discoursing, unconsciously perhaps, but glibly, in the motley language, the novelty of which had so shocked them on their first arrival.

There are of course some few exceptions to this general rule—I myself, for instance, reader! I have been addressing you continuously for some hours, and till now you have not once heard the word "Pucka."

"Pucka" is an adjective, and when applied to a road, it means that it is a metalled one; when to a wall, that it is of solid masonry—no lath-and-plaster erection; to a fruit, that it is ripe; to a scoundrel or a Kashmiri, that he is an out-and-out one, &c. &c. It is diametrically opposed to everything that is "Brummagem," which, in the mouth of the Anglo-Indian, would be called "kutcha;" for "kutcha" is the antipodes of "pucka." But "pucka" has many other meanings, and is used as an expletive, when the Anglo-Indian wishes to be particularly impressive; for instance, his *protégé* is a "pucka fine fellow." Combinations, too, can be made of the two words, and it is possible for a man or a thing to be "pucka-kutcha," or "kutcha-pucka," as the case may be; but the meaning of this last barbarism I am unable to explain, and rejoice to say that it is not an epithet of frequent occurrence, its perpetrators being usually men of a bygone age, now rapidly dying out; and whatever may be their after-fate, we will hope that the place of their abode may be situate at a distance from that of the shade of Lindley Murray: to be sentenced to hear an eternity of lectures on solecisms made by them in a former state would be an awful doom.

I never use the word "pucka" without compunction, for it ever calls up to my memory a hot evening in the courtyard of the King's Palace at Lucknow. A palanquin, with bearers ready to start, a wan and worn, yet handsome face, with big, fever-lit eyes that looked beseechingly at me, and a feeble but earnest voice which said, as a slender hand wrung mine—"Good bye, dear fellow; you are going to be foolish enough to spend some years in this —— country. Now, let me beg of you, let nothing ever induce you to call anything 'pucka,' and for Heaven's sake, old boy, never take beer to anybody else's wine!!"

These were the parting words of a brother officer, who was then starting "homeward bound" in the autumn of 1858, for the doctors had said that nothing but the pure air of his native land could restore health to his enfeebled frame, worn out by climate, exposure, and the hardships of the campaign.

Soap and Deuce were the names of our two next halting-places, names certainly in a manner appropriate, for to judge from the neutral tint of dirt that pervaded everything and everybody, the deuce of a bit of soap was there to be found in either.

The track which we followed led us along pleasant little sequestered valleys, well-watered, and in parts well-cultivated—although the richness of the soil is a premium on lazy husbandry—and shut in on all sides by low hills covered with dense forest. It was the perfection of sylvan scenery. After leaving Deuce, we began to ascend; the valley rapidly narrowed; sycamore, walnut, apple, and pear tree gave place to the lofty pine; all trace of cultivation vanished; and before us rose the steep sides of the mountain ridge on which, said our guides, we must halt that night. It was a steep and weary climb, but the scenery around was magnificent; and ever as we ascended, the low hills beneath us dwindled into insignificance, and no longer obstructed the view; beyond them, as though at our feet, stretched the vale of Kashmir.

Soon the pine-trees, even, ceased to shadow our path; a belt of stunted birch-trees was all that remained between us and the bare hill-side: this passed, our climb was nearly at an end. We were now above the tree line, and to the right and left stretched the skeleton backbone of the ridge; in front, a wall of rock rose almost perpendicularly; up this led the track we were to follow on the morrow, and beyond it lay the much-vaunted hunting-grounds.

It was bitterly cold; a keen wind sprung up—tents, coolies, and baggage were far behind, so we crouched under a fragment of rock, and gazed regretfully at the now far distant "happy valley," which shone like an emerald in the warm light of the evening sun, whose rays, alas! reached not us. Soon, however, dim forms begin to appear wearily wending their upward way through the birch-trees below us, and the welcome sound of the voice of Ali Bux, raised in wrath, strikes on our ear. In due course of time the tents are pitched and fires lighted, and at last dinner is announced to be ready by the mumbling voice of my khitmutghar, "Busharat" (a name which, being interpreted, signifies "good tidings"), and never (methought on that occasion) was appellation more apt.

The night was piercingly cold, and directly after dinner we turned in. I was roused from my first slumber by one of my "shikarrees," who came to tell me that if I would start with him a few hours before dawn he would show me no end of bears; "but don't tell the other Sahibs," added the rascal, in a stage whisper. I grumbled a reluctant consent, and turning round, proceeded to make the most of the few hours of sleep that were left me. Between two and three o'clock next morning I stole from my tent with a noiseless tread, and started with my three shikarrees up the rocky pass. It was freezing hard, and the moon threw a bright but deceptive light on our path. On reaching the summit, I almost forgave my attendant Kashmiris for having waked me so soon, and the sluggard regrets I had been indulging in during the steep climb vanished, for—

> "Lo! the ethereal cliffs
> Of Caucasus, whose icy summits shone
> Among the stars like sunlight, and around
> Whose caverned base"—

rolled like waves the dark indistinct forms of rounded mountain ridges, mounting higher and higher, till they seemed to break in foam on the shores of perpetual snow. It was a scene of almost unearthly beauty. Never even on the clearest day have I seen the jagged peaks so distinctly visible as on that night, when, crowned with stars and lit up by the moonlight, they stood out bold and prominent from their dark background of cloud.

We now passed over a wide plain that sloped downwards before us into blue mist; a scanty herbage covered it, and here and there a stunted bush grew, or a quaintly-shaped mass of rock lay half buried. We were getting very near the bear warren, said my guide.

At last the sound of a small stream reached our ears, and now we must halt and wait for daylight. Thick clouds by this time obscured the moon, and cast a black shadow on all around; two of the shikarrees laid themselves down and slept while the other kept watch, peering steadily through the darkness, and I paced briskly up and down in the vain endeavour to keep warm, and "longed for day." It seemed as though morn would never come! At last, in the eastern horizon, a faint glimmer, which gradually stole along the snowy peaks, made its welcome appearance; the sleepers are roused, and with cautious step and slow we move down towards the stream, which now, as it grows lighter, we can see meandering along below us; big boulders of rock, and here and there patches of green grass, cover its banks; it is on these patches that Bruin loves to feed.

We clumsily allowed ourselves to be heard or seen by the first bear we came upon, for he was shambling off at a canter, well out of shot ere we caught sight of him; but we were afterwards more successful, and about eleven o'clock the whole party met at breakfast on the banks of the stream, very well satisfied with their sport, with the world in general, and with themselves and their rifles in particular.

We pitched camp a few miles down the stream, and halted there next day, bent on making the most of our time.

The number of bears that we saw during these two days was quite surprising! On one occasion, when stalking a monstrous fellow who was grazing a few hundred yards away from me, I took advantage of a slight inequality in the ground, which hid me from him, to shoulder my rifle and run on towards him, keeping my eye fixed on the brow of the little rise before me, over which I every moment expected to see his big form appearing. Whilst running on thus, another bear rose from under my very feet; I had literally kicked him up as one would a hare. He was fortunately quite as much startled at my apparition as I was at his; evinced, I am glad to say, no wish to dispute my right to stand on his "native heath," and scampered off, rolling and tumbling down the slope in ludicrous haste.

I put a bullet into him as he went; but it had only the effect of accelerating his movements, and of frightening the bear I had been bent on circumventing. And that same evening, when obliged to leave off shooting, as I was at a distance from camp and night coming on, there were within sight of me no less than *four* bears, each peaceably feeding on his little patch of green grass.

On the same day, the "official friend," after a successful morning's beat, felt his old enemy, intermittent fever, threatening him, and wended his way back to camp, not a little disgusted at finding himself obliged to "lay up" at so inopportune a moment. His relentless foe followed him, and folding him in an icy embrace, wrestled with him there, and threw him on his bed shivering in an ague fit. After a time this passed off, and the victim fell into a doze, from which an unusual stir in the little camp aroused him. "A bear, sahib; a bear close to the tent;" and crawling from under his blankets, he stalked and killed the animal within sight of camp.

I think I have said enough to show that our

sport was not bad. The brown bear is hardly so large as his black brother, and much less fierce. We were none of us once charged by a wounded bear; though more than once they turned round on us with angry intention, but never summoned up pluck actually to make a rush. Their colour varies from dark brown to almost a dirty white; the skins are very handsome, and the fur is long and thick. All we shot were in capital condition, and the amount of bear's grease—which we left for eagles and carrion crows to fatten upon—would make the fortune of a hairdresser.

We left the land of bears on the 23rd September; and crossing some high ridges, descended an interminable hill-side into a warmer climate, and halted eventually in a pleasant valley, close to a little village called Chind. We next day followed the windings of the valley, which were very beautiful, to the village of Mogul Maidan. During this march we had some good "chukor" shooting, and found teal in plenty near the stream.

From Mogul Maidan to Doda, where we found the rest of our camp awaiting us, is about thirty miles, to accomplish which distance took us three days. The path led us over a continuous succession of lofty mountain ridges divided by deep valleys, and the whole covered with dense forest. From the summits of these ridges magnificent views of the snowy range are obtained. Of these the finest and most extensive is the one which shows you in mid distance, but far below your feet, the fertile valley of Kishtawar. From this the gaze travels up and up, higher and still higher, over range above range of mountain, some with scarped sides of grey granite, others of red sandstone, casting deeper shadows from their fissured and weather-beaten flanks; while others present a seemingly endless slope of dark pine forest. Here the eye would willingly linger, sated with the variety of beauty thus offered to its view, unconscious of the arctic world above—the glaciers and the snowy peaks which, clad in robes of virgin snow, soar like clouds in heaven's blue vault.

The artist looks and looks in rapt and ever-increasing wonderment; then searches for some object near at hand, by comparison with which to mete out, as it were, into a series of views, the stupendousness of the scene. Just below him a giant pine-tree, withered by fire, stretches his blackened trunk aloft, and waves his scathed arms in space like a Titan struck by a thunderbolt from heaven; lifeless, yet in death defiant. This shall be his guide; this shall frame his panorama of height. Vain resolve. The topmost branch reaches not the base even of that ethereal fairyland of snow; the pine-tree is just one world too short for his purpose.

We had at first intended to pass through the city Kishtawah, and pay a visit to the veteran Baste Ram; but the valley looked so hot, and the mountain breezes were so charmingly cool, that we took the upper road.

Doda is a town of some size, built on the banks of our old friend, the Chenab. It possesses a fort, in which are imprisoned some State offenders of royal blood, whose wives and families are, by a refinement of cruelty, permitted to reside in a house which is clearly visible from the prison, but to whom all communication with its unhappy inmates is denied.

We crossed the Chenab next day by a swinging rope bridge; and after an easy march of about eleven miles, halted in a beautiful valley covered with rice and corn fields, and orchards of pear and apple trees, intersected here and there by strips of as yet unreclaimed forest-land, jutting out from the dark belt of foliage that fenced the valley in.

The town of Buddrawah—a place of some importance—was our next halting-place. It is picturesquely situated; and the pears and apples grown in its gardens surpassed in flavour and excellence those of Kashmir itself. A considerable shawl manufacture is carried on here, but the goods are of a very coarse texture.

The Puddree-Dhar Pass tried our powers of climbing next day; and the descent on the opposite side is very difficult walking. Three marches brought us to the banks of the Sion river—a stream of some magnitude; this we crossed by means of "deris," or inflated skins; and on the opposite bank found a gay cavalcade awaiting us. The party proved to be some of the retainers of the Rajah of Chumba, a small hill state, at whose capital we were to pass the night. His Rajahship, hearing of our approach, had sent horses to carry, and servants to escort, us with all due honour to his palace.

The path was steep and narrow, and it was not without grave apprehensions that I mounted a fat, pink-nosed white steed of some sixteen hands, with tail and mane dyed red, caparisoned in native style, with a carcase like a dray horse, but with the longest, thinnest, and most rickety legs that horse was ever cursed with.

The catastrophe I dreaded soon occurred: my fidgety Bucephalus soon got a hind leg over the precipice, and after a vain effort to recover his footing, fell backwards down the steep hill-side. Fortunately for me, his brief struggle gave me time to slip off his back on to the footway, before he took such a very unpleasantly short cut to the bottom.

After an ascent of some miles we descended into the valley of the Ravee, and marched up the right bank of that beautiful stream till the town of Chumba came in sight.

The town is built on a rock, which towers to a

great height above the river, and is connected with the mainland by two bridges of lengthy deodar beams; a broad paved road leads up to the plateau on which the town is built. It consists of about 1000 houses; and a level greensward, about five hundred yards long by eighty broad, has been left unbuilt upon in the centre. Here the young men and boys are ever playing "hockey,"* while the grey-bearded seniors sit at

* Hockey! The youth of Chumba play genuine hockey on foot, but the game as practised by their forefathers must have been a much more exciting one.—Vide Cunningham's *Ladak*, pp. 311, 312.

"The favourite amusement of the Botis, both of Ladák and of Balti, is *Polo,* in which all parties, from the highest to the lowest, can take a part. I saw the game played at Mulbil, in a field 400 yards long and 80 yards broad, which was walled round for the purpose with a stone dyke. There were twenty players on each side, all mounted on ponies and armed with sticks about four feet long, and bent at the lower end. One player took the ball and advanced alone into the middle of the field, where he threw up the ball, and as it fell, struck it towards one of the goals. The goals were formed of two upright stones placed about twenty-five or thirty feet apart. When the ball was driven through a goal, one of the successful party was obliged to dismount and pick it up, for if the opposite party should have driven it back before it was picked up, the goal did not count. The game consisted in winning a certain number of their shop doors and look on. To the left are some Hindoo temples of great antiquity, and the Rajah's palace and gardens, which, though small, are tastefully laid out. We found tents ready pitched for us in these gardens, and at the request of our servants, who wanted rest, agreed to halt there the next day.

Next day we paid a visit of ceremony to the Rajah to thank him for all his courtesies. He

goals, either five, seven, or nine. Numerous musicians were in attendance, who made a most lively din whenever a goal was won; and the noise was increased by the cheers of the successful party.

"The game is a very spirited one, and well calculated for the display of bold and active horsemanship.* Accidental blows occur frequently, but the poor ponies are the principal sufferers. The game was once common in India under the name of *Chaogan*, but it is now completely forgotten. The old chaogan-grounds still exist in every large town in the Panjàb hills; in Bilâspur, Nadon, Shujanpur, Kangra, Haripur, and Chamba, where the goal-stones are still standing. The game is repeatedly mentioned by Bâber; but after his time it gradually became obsolete. It was introduced by the Musalman conquerors, and the very first king, Kutb-ud-din Aibak, was killed by a fall from his horse when playing

* "It is well and tersely described by Vigne as 'hockey on horseback.' Mr. Thornton calls it '*cricket* on horseback;' but it has nothing whatever in common with cricket."

sent his own elephants to convey us in the most dignified (and uncomfortable) way to his palace, and on arrival we were ushered up a dark, narrow, winding staircase, into a little plain whitewashed room, at the door of which we were met by a fat, uninteresting-looking boy of eighteen, who insisted on shaking hands with us, and, to our surprise, kept his shoes on. It was the Rajah! who, we were afterwards told, prided himself on his disregard for the formalities of Eastern etiquette;

at chaogan in A.D. 1210.* The Pathán kings of India still continued to join in the game down to the time of Sikander Lodi, in A.D. 1498, when 'one day, while the king and his court were playing at chaogan, the bat of Haibat Khan Shirwani by accident came in contact with the head of Suliman, the son of Darya Khan Lodi, who received a severe blow. This was resented on the spot by Khizr Khan, the brother of Suliman, who, galloping up to Haibat Khan, struck him violently over the skull. In a few minutes both sides joined in the quarrel, and the field was in uproar and confusion. Mahmud Khan Lodi and Khan Khanan Lodi interposing, endeavoured to pacify Haibat Khan, and succeeded in persuading him to go home quietly with them. The king, apprehensive of conspiracy, retired immediately to the palace; but nothing more transpiring, he made another party at the same game a few days after.'"†

* "Briggs's Ferishta," I. p. 199. † "Idem," p. 574.

the pert, awkward manner he affected in their place was as offensive as it was ludicrous.

Our host then waddled back to his arm-chair, before which was a round table, laid out with paper, pens, ink, and a most business-like-looking despatch-box, and pointing to three chairs placed in a row on his right, asked us to be seated.

The conversation soon flagged, for the Rajah was not amusing, till one of us, happening to look at his watch, the potentate grew suddenly loquacious; watches seemed to be his hobby, and he examined ours and compared them with his own with great seeming interest. He could talk no language but his own, but told us that he regularly took in the English papers, and had them translated to him, thus obtaining, said he, intelligence of all that was going on direct from England.

We asked to see one of his latest papers, and he handed us with great pride a *Taranaki Herald*, nine months old. His English news therefore came to him direct *viâ New Zealand!*

From Chumba to Kangra took us five days. I was, I confess, disappointed with the Kangra valley; to a person coming from the plains it must be, no doubt, a very striking scene, but to the traveller who marches thither from Kashmir, its beauties—for it has many—seem very second-rate. The town of Kangra is without exception the cleanest, or, more properly speaking, the only clean Oriental town I ever saw.

The fort is built on an oblong rock, isolated from, but commanded by, the surrounding heights. The Ben Gunga, "a river at all times breast deep," washes its base on three sides; on the fourth a deep dell divides it from the neighbouring mountain. It is well supplied with water, affords accommodation for a large garrison, and against an Oriental foe may be looked on as impregnable.

From Kangra to Simla, *viâ* Jowalli-mookhi* and Belaspore, but little occurred worth mentioning. At the first stage we said good-bye to the Major, who started off by palanquin dâk to the plains, and we pushed on by forced marches, for we were pressed for time, to Belaspore. Here we

* Jowalli-mookhi.—Vide Thornton's *Gazetteer*. Thornton spells the word *Jewale*-mukh.

recrossed the Sutlej, grown into a mighty stream, and lost poor Noura, who, while bathing in its waters, was swept away by the current and seen no more; and on the 16th October, exactly three months from the date of our departure, the "official friend" and I rode into Simla.

Our happy holiday was over!

APPENDIX.

APPENDIX.

I.

Extract from Memorandum drawn up by the order of Colonel A. Scott Waugh, Engineers, Surveyor-General of India, F.R.S., F.R.G.S., &c., on the Progress of the Kashmir Series of the G. T. Survey of India; with Observations on the late Conquest of Gilgit, and other Incidental Matters, by Captain S. G. Montgomerie, Engineers, F.G.S., &c., in charge of the Series.

WITH reference to my last memorandum on the great flood of the river Indus, I have not as yet been able to obtain any further information as to its origin, though the expedition against Gilgit has succeeded, as I anticipated it would.

The Maharajah has directed every inquiry to be made, and I hope to be able to give a correct account of the origin of the flood when I return to the Maharajah's territories next year. Meantime, the expedition has confirmed several important points in the geography of the countries near Gilgit, and a short account of the expedition itself may be interesting.

The Maharajah laid in a large supply of food at the forts of Astor and Boonjee during the summer of 1859. Hitherto, one of the greatest obstacles to making a successful attack on Gilgit has been the difficulties of getting supplies. The natives are in the habit of using the old expression, to the effect that a small force going against Gilgit was sure to be defeated, and a large force to be starved. To obviate this, a hundred ponies were put at each of the seventeen halting-places between Kashmir and Boonjee, *viâ* Gurais and Astor, and whilst the weather permitted, one hundred loads of grain were delivered daily at Boonjee.

In June—July of this year, several detachments of Sepoys were moved upon Gilgit, mustering finally at Boonjee to about 4000 men, under Colonel Devi Singh and Colonel Dooloo Singh. The whole body then advanced upon Gilgit, crossing the Indus by means of a boat; further on they crossed a tributary river by a wooden bridge. No opposition was met before reaching Gilgit itself, and there the Gilgities got inside their fort and held out for a short time, during which there was a little firing on both sides, ending by the Gilgities surrendering, the Maharajah's force losing one man by the bursting of a gun, and the Gilgities leaving one dead man in the fort, supposed to have died a natural death during the siege.

Having settled affairs at Gilgit, the force advanced further up the valley to Shirni (or Shirwat) fort, where there was some slight resistance, ending as before in capitulation. The force then advanced on Yasseen, which is on the Gilgit river, and not on a separate tributary of the Indus. Yasseen fell into the hands of the force, and the son of the Goraman, who had held Gilgit in addition to Yasseen, made his escape over the mountains to the west and on into Badakhshan. The Goraman himself died during 1857. He was well known in the whole of the country between the Indus and Cabul, and was generally called an Adamkhor, or man-eater, from a habit that he had of catching all strangers that he could, for the purpose of exchanging them for the large dogs so much prized in that part of the world. The Goraman and his son had till this year held Yasseen, and for a short time Gilgit also, though once or twice driven out from the latter by the Dogras. In addition to the main body of the Dogra force advancing from the south, an armed body of Baltis advanced through Shigar, and thence by the Nagar and Hoonza valleys, threatening Gilgit on the east.

Another force was to have advanced from the west

under the instructions of an agent from Dheer and Chitraul, but it was not apparently in time, though possibly the mere talk of it made the Goraman's son unhappy as to his line of retreat.

This conquest, which may be said to have been made without loss of life, is highly creditable to the Maharajah, and his officers who planned and carried it out. The effects are, in some respects, likely to be very salutary. In the first place, the mere fact of having a force in Gilgit overawes and keeps in check the robber clans of Nagar and Hoonza, who have for years infested the roads between Balti and Ladak on the one side, and Yarkund on the other; and latterly to such an extent, that those roads in their immediate neighbourhoods, though the shortest, have been almost completely closed to anything in the shape of a merchant. Keeping possession of Gilgit during the cold weather, when all communication with Kashmir is closed, has always been the most difficult business. The Maharajah has, however, left nearly 3000 men in the valley, and consequently in future it is to be hoped that they will hold their own, and that the traffic from Skardo direct to Yarkund will again be resumed.

In the second place, this successful expedition has had a very wholesome effect on all the petty tribes lying between Gilgit and the Cabul territories, and ultimately may be of assistance in keeping the Swat valley in check, Swat being still one of the recusant tribes on our north-west frontier.

At the durbars of the Maharajah during this season, men from Chitraul, Dheer, Swat, Kholi, Palus, &c., were in attendance, as well as those from Chilas, Nagar, and Hoonza, who have been constant attendants for some years.

At the last durbar held by the Maharajah, Colonel Devi Sing made his salaam, having just returned from the Gilgit expedition. Some of the Yasseen men were introduced at the same time. One long brass gun, of about 3 lbs. bore, accompanied the Colonel, his Sepoys having taken it from the Goraman's son. This gun seemed to be well cast, and had a Persian inscription on it, to the effect that it was made in Budakshan, or had belonged to that place. Among the minor results of the expedition was a great influx of presents to the Maharajah from all the chiefs between Gilgit and Kafiristan. Perhaps the most valuable in the eyes of the Curator of the Asiatic Society's Museum would have been a splendid live male specimen of the markhor, the greatest prize of Himalayan sportsmen. This animal was introduced into the full durbar, guided by four men with guy ropes. It was really a handsome animal, of a light fawn-colour, with a capital pair of horns, and a fine long beard. The top of the markhor's head was perhaps 5½ feet from the ground, the horns towering up above all the men in attendance. The keepers of this animal evidently held him in the greatest respect, though he had been a captive for at least two months. This markhor was a present from the chiefs of Kholi and Palus, on the Indus.

The Chilasses sent in some very fine half-domesticated goats, a part of which the Maharajah distributed amongst the European visitors to Kashmir. One of these goats, now in my possession, has a very fine pair of horns of the markhor kind.

The country on either side of the Indus, between the British district of Huzara and the Maharajah's valley of Astor, has hitherto been all but impassable. With Chilas, Kholi, and Palus all under the orders of the Maharajah, a very slight pressure ought to open out the remainder, down to the Huzara district, which might tend to bring the Akhoon of Swat to reason. At the same time, opening out the whole valley of the Indus is in itself no small advantage, if it will enable travellers to pass along in safety.

Traffic will undoubtedly increase, and, moreover, the Punjab Government will have the means of getting full information, in case the Indus should again be blocked up in any part of its course. In the latter respect, the conquest of Gilgit, with Yasseen, Hoonza, and Nagar, is really very valuable, as it places under a friendly Native State the only great tributary of the Indus concerning which the British Government has hitherto been unable to get any reliable information. This tributary, moreover, is, in my opinion, the one on which the late great flood of the Indus was generated.

If these countries are in thorough subjection to the Maharajah, such a calamity as the cataclysm of 1858 ought not again to befal British subjects on the Indus, without their having, at any rate, full warning, even if it were not possible to prevent or mitigate it by the scientific application of labour, as it most probably would be.

II.

Letter from the Deputy-Commissioner of Simla to the Secretary to the Government of the Punjab, dated the 14th September, 1861, relating to the Murder of the late Adolphe Schlagentweit.

I HAVE the honour to report, for the information of his Honour the Lieutenant-Governor, that I have at this moment in my possession the Journal of Mr. Adolphe Schlagentweit, who, his Honour doubtless recollects, was so cruelly murdered at Kashgar in 1857. I have also what is alleged to be his skull.

2. On my arrival at Leh in August last, one Mirza Abdool Wudud, a man of Herat, presented himself at my tent, and stated that in a caravan expected shortly at Leh from Yarkund there was a parcel to his address containing a manuscript book, which belonged to the gentleman who was put to death at Kashgar, as well as what he fully believed to be his skull. The Mirza represented himself to be entirely without funds, and despaired of ever recovering the parcel from the men in charge of the caravan.

I lost no time in despatching the Mirza with a Tartar

servant of mine towards Yarkund, with instructions to take the parcel, paying for its carriage, and to follow me with as much speed as possible to Sreenuggur.

3. About the eighth march from Leh they met the caravan. The persons in charge at first positively declined to give up the parcel; they then demanded two hundred rupees; eventually they agreed to take six gold mohurs, worth seventeen rupees each, all the money my servant had with him. The Mirza and servant at once started for Sreenuggur, which they reached with the precious parcel a few days after myself.

4. The Mirza's account of himself is that he left Herat about five years ago in consequence of the disturbed state of the town, and has been wandering ever since in the countries between Afghanistan and Yarkund in the guise of a Hakeem, or physician. At Bokhara he heard of the death of Mr. Schlagentweit. Aware of the value which would be attached by us to any books, papers, &c., belonging to the unfortunate traveller, the Mirza, on his arrival at Kashgar, set diligently to work to search for his property. For a long time he was unsuccessful, but about sixteen months ago he contrived to procure, through one Kurreem Khan, son of a Moolla (or priest) of Kashgar, a manuscript book which a dealer in snuff had bought for the sake of the paper, which

he used in packing small quantities of snuff.* Something less than one rupee was paid for the book.

Not long after, a cultivator informed the Mirza that after Mr. Schlagentweit was put to death, his head was first suspended over a bridge, and then placed in a tree under which he happened to grow melons, and that he buried it in his field. The Mirza dug up the ground, which was then covered with snow at the spot indicated, and found a skull. The Mirza is confident that it is really the skull of the murdered man; but I am not very sanguine in the matter, and shall not be certain as to its genuineness till I have submitted it to a competent judge. The book† contains 131 pages of closely written notes in the German language, and is Mr. Schlagentweit's journal from the 14th of June to the 11th of August, the day he started from Kargalik, a village fourteen miles on the Ladak side of Yarkund.

5. With regard to the manner of his death, the Mirza's account agrees in every material point with that given by Kashmiri Abdulla, and published in Messrs. H. and R. Schlagentweit's printed Circular.

On arriving near the city of Yarkund, Mr. Schlagen-

* The Bhoj Putta or Birch bark is generally used by retail snuff-dealers.

† I shall despatch this book by Overland Mail to care of Messrs. H. and R. Schlagentweit's agents in London.

weit found it closely besieged by a robber chief or crescentader of Kokand named Dilla Khan. By this man Mr. Schlagentweit was made a prisoner. Almost immediately after Dilla Khan was compelled by the Chinese to fall back on Kashgar, also a Chinese town, but which had been occupied by another "crescentader" of Kokand named Khoja Vulli Khan, Mr. Schlagentweit continued a prisoner in the hands of Dilla Khan, and was brought to Kashgar. On reaching a spot not more than two hundred yards from the tents of the Khoja Vulli Khan, one of Mr. Schlagentweit's guard went to inquire of him what was to be done with the "Feringhee." The Khoja, who is described to be a man of infamous character, at once ordered his execution. The persons entrusted with this work endeavoured to bind Mr. Schlagentweit's arms, but this indignity he successfully resisted. A blow was then struck with a sword, which took effect under his right ear. Another was aimed at the left side of his head, but neither proving fatal his throat was cut with a knife which one of the executioners drew from his side. The head was then severed from the body and hung up over a bridge.

The Khoja was soon after driven out of Kashgar by the Chinese, and is now wandering about a miserable drunkard without a single follower.

6. With reference to the above narrative, I think it right to mention that it does differ in one or two points from the account given by intelligent persons at the time residing in Yarkund. *There* the story is that Mr. Schlagentweit made friends with Khoja Dilla Khan, and offered to direct his operations against Yarkund, that he was forced to fly with the defeated Khoja, and that he was put to death by Khoja Vulli Khan for sitting before him in a disrespectful attitude.* My informant, the Mirza, however, states that Mr. Schlagentweit was never in the presence of Khoja Vulli Khan, while with regard to his directing the operations against Yarkund it is possible that he may have offered to assist Dilla Khan, but certainly not till he was taken prisoner and saw that his life was in danger.

7. With respect to the chances of recovering any other articles, the property of Mr. Schlagentweit, I am of opinion that little or no hope can reasonably be entertained of any further success. The Mirza informs me that he left no stone unturned in his search at Kashgar, but never succeeded in obtaining the trace even of anything besides the book; and this is, however, the less to be regretted, if it should prove true that

* That is, with the soles of his feet turned towards the Khoja.

Mr. Schlagentweit* sent all his journals up to the 14th June to Kangra.

8. In conclusion, I have only to express a warm hope that Mirza Abdul Wudud will not be left unrewarded.† To his exertions we owe the rescue from destruction of a valuable manuscript, rendered doubly valuable by the tragic death of its writer, one of the boldest, most enterprising, and accomplished travellers of modern times.

P.S.—I avail myself of this opportunity to state with reference to a repeated assertion to the contrary, which appears in the printed reports relating to Mr. Schlagentweit's death, that I never to my knowledge saw Mahomed Ameer, and certainly never recommended him to Mr. A. Schlagentweit. I believe that he was a most useful and faithful servant.

* Dr. Hurkishen states that he received a letter from Mr. A. Schlagentweit, dated the 14th June, 1857, in which he mentions having sent two Dâk parcels for transmission to Kangra. (See printed circular.) The parcels never came to hand, nor does any inquiry appear to have been made respecting their fate. This is unfortunate; even now it is not too late.

(Signed) W. Hay.

† Besides defraying the Mirza's expenses from Leh to Cashmere, I have made him an allowance of a rupee a day from my private purse. He accompanies me to Simla.

Letter No. 1961, *dated* 21*st September*, 1861, *from Secretary to Government, Punjab, to Lord W. Hay, Deputy Commissioner of Simla.*

I am directed to acknowledge your letter of the 14th instant, and to convey the thanks of the Honourable the Lieutenant-Governor for your exertions in procuring the manuscript journal of the late Mr. A. Schlagentweit.

2. His Honour authorizes a reward of 500 rupees being given to the Mirza on his arriving at Simla, in addition to his expenses being paid from the time he joined you at Leh, and sanctions the money advanced to the Mirza being reimbursed to yourself. You are requested to submit a bill for the whole amount for the counter-signature of this office.

3. I am to add that a copy of your letter and this reply will be forwarded to the Supreme Government, with a request that they will communicate the same to the family of the late Mr. Schlagentweit at Berlin, and with a suggestion that your letter may be published in the *Calcutta Gazette.*

III.

The "Hindostan and Thibet" Road, commonly called the "New Road."

THIS is a noble, though unfinished work, and bears powerful testimony to the vigour and prescience of the Marquis of Dalhousie's Administration; to its vigour, as being a striking proof of what engineering skill, unthwarted by a false economy, can effect; to its prescience, as being a manifest sign of the great commercial projects, in connexion with China, entertained by that able Governor-General of India.

The present road was actually commenced by Colonel Kennedy, of the Royal army, aided by other officers, in the year 1850, although before this two other attempts to trace a road had been made under different auspices. Both these, however, were eventually abandoned, it being evident that the line taken by them was not calculated to combine the two great desiderata of hill roads—viz., (1) the avoidance of *steep inclines;* (2) the avoidance of *unnecessary detour*, or the keeping as nearly as practicable to the direct line. The first of these requisites, indeed, they both succeeded in attaining in a remarkable degree; but of the second they appear to have lost sight altogether. The old Hill Road, despite its narrowness, despite its rugged descents and precipitous declivities, would have been preferred by the traveller—so preposterously long were the weary windings of its scientifically laid-out rivals.

The New Road, as it at present exists, reaches from Kalka, at the foot of the hills, to a few miles beyond Serahun, in the hill state of Bussahir, a distance of 177¼ miles. From this point to Shipkee, on the western frontier of China—to which station the road was originally intended to reach—is a distance of 93 miles; one-third, therefore, of the great work remains uncompleted. The ground has been, however, surveyed, and the line of road partly traced.

The events of 1857, the great mutiny year, put a stop to further progress, and since then Government has not thought fit to grant the necessary funds requisite to cover the expense of future operations.

The road from Kalka to Simla is in many parts quite level, but in general rises at the slight incline of 1 foot in 33,* save in one place near Dugshai, where a ridge

* "The maximum gradient observed was 1 foot in 30, at which about one-fifth of the distance was laid out; over three-fifths of the distance a gradient of 1 foot in 33 was observed, and the remaining one-fifth remained level."—*Vide Briggs' Report.*

has to be surmounted. Here the ascent is comparatively steep (9 feet in 100 feet).

This ridge Captain Briggs, successor of Kennedy, proposed to tunnel through, and actually commenced the work in January, 1855. It was continued till 1858 by him and his successors, but, owing to want of funds, progress since that year has been stopped.

The total length of the Dugshai tunnel when completed will be 1950 feet.

On the north, or Simla side, 700 feet of tunnelling has already been completed, of which 240 feet is lined with solid masonry. On the south side, a length of 400 feet has been excavated, leaving 850 feet of tunnel unfinished. The cost of this undertaking, as far as it has gone, has been 1627*l.* 8*s.* The distance saved by this tunnel, when completed, will be two miles, two furlongs, and one hundred yards.

There is also another tunnel on the Upper Road a few miles north of Simla. This is 560 feet in length, and is cut through solid rock.

There are branch roads to the military stations of Kussowlie, Subathao, and Dugshai, and at intervals along the road are commodious staging bungalows, or houses of rest, for the accommodation of travellers.

The distance from Kalka to Simla by the Hindostan and Thibet road is 54¼ miles; add to this the branches to Kussowlie, Subathoa, and Dugshai, and the total amount of fair carriage road, from 14 to 16 feet broad, with substantial parapets where the precipices are very abrupt, is 72 miles. This was effected at a total cost of about 32,500*l.*, including the expenses attendant on the erection of the staging bungalows.

After leaving Simla, the road ceases to be available for carriages, and dwindles to a breadth of 6 feet; it is, however, much more level, and for ponies and other beasts of burden, and for travellers, either on foot or horseback, is a most safe, as well as pleasant, means of communication with the interior.

From Simla to seven miles beyond Serahun is a distance of 123 miles; of this at least two-thirds is perfectly level. It was constructed at a cost of about 25,000*l.*, including twelve good staging bungalows.

To give an adequate idea of the difficulties attendant on a work of this description, it is necessary to attempt to convey a notion of the shape of the ground over which a nearly level road has to be constructed.

The Himalayas consist of a vast system of water-courses, or river-beds, now narrow and rocky, and again spreading out into small valleys, divided by spurs or ridges of hills, more or less broken or precipitous, whose summits form the watershed line of the numberless rills which spring from their sides, and whose drainage feeds them. These small spurs are offshoots again from larger spurs, which in their turn stretch out from mightier ridges still, from the giant ribs of the snow-clad backbone, which they help to prop up.

It is manifest, therefore, that in laying out a tolerably level road across this interminable succession of hill and valley, the idea of going straight must be abandoned, unless the employers of the engineer are prepared to meet the cost of a road consisting, with but few exceptional intervals, of tunnel and viaduct, viaduct and tunnel. And for the same reason it becomes evident that one of the large ribs of mountain before mentioned must be selected as the base of operations.

This was the plan adopted by Colonel Kennedy, and a ridge suitable to his purpose was discovered, which stretched out from the western extremity of the outer chain of the Himalayas, forming the watershed of the rivers Sutlej and Pubur, and reaching to the plains in the vicinity of Kalka. Along this ridge the road winds until the ridge itself ceases to preserve its identity amid the stupendous labyrinth of lofty peaks in which it loses itself; and at this point it was found necessary to cross the Sutlej at Wangtoo, and take advantage of the valley of Kunawur as the line for further operations.

So much for the theory of hill road-making. It need hardly be added that to put this theory in practice is no easy task, but one which tries to the utmost not only the professional skill, but the physical strength and courage of the engineer, who must add to his scientific attainments the firm foot, cool head, and muscular power of the mountaineer — the mighty ridge along whose rugged sides he must lay out his road has not the complaisance to mount up gradually to the parent chain from which it springs at an easy incline and with a grassy slope—it, on the contrary, puts every possible obstacle in the way of the mathematical line he must trace—it is for ever changing its character, turning off to the right and left without apparent cause, and presents a different elevation at every one of its windings. It is now of friable sandstone, and again of stratified rock—now it opposes masses of gneiss, now walls of granite, and again beds of argillaceous slate to his progress—it is as capricious as a woman and as stubborn as a mule!

There are two ways of overcoming these obstacles—by excavation and blasting, or by simply going round or avoiding them. The former mode of operation being necessarily much the most expensive, the latter is almost invariably adopted, except when it happens to involve too great a deviation from the general directness of the line; and the consequence is, that the new, scientifically-planned Machiavelian line of level road from Kalka to Simla is eleven miles longer than the old steep, up-hill and down-dale, simple-minded, cross-country mode of communication.

A similar difference in length between the new and old road is observable beyond Simla; the disparity of distance is not, however, quite so great, being only about twenty miles in the whole distance of 123.

The Hindostan and Thibet road is in excellent order, and is kept in thorough repair at a most trifling cost. The expenses attendant on keeping the carriage-road in a state of great efficiency have been for the last five years only 5*l.* per mile per annum, including the necessary repairs to the numerous bridges and viaducts; and the annual repairs to the road north of Simla have been carried out at a cost of only 2*l.* per mile per annum.

I am indebted for the above facts to the kindness of Captain Houchen, who has for some years past held the responsible appointment of Superintendent of Hill Roads.

The New Road, in common with all other projects, great or small, has its friends and its enemies, and is advocated by the one party as strongly as it is condemned by the other.

The arguments *pro* and *con* may be summed up in a few words.

If your object is to effect a communication with China for commercial purposes, say the opposition, why go so far north? Why not make Darjeeling or Mussouri your starting-point? Darjeeling is nearly equidistant from Calcutta, the metropolis of Bengal, and Lhassa, the metropolis of Chinese Tartary; and the line which would connect these two capital cities in the most direct manner is surely the one to choose. Mussouri is certainly more out of the way, and possesses in a minor degree the advantages of position which Darjeeling offers; but a line *viâ* Mussouri, over the pass, would connect Delhi, one of the richest cities of the plains, with China, and is clearly preferable to one farther north, which, after winding its weary length across the mountain barrier of the Himalayas, *debouches* at a point on the borders of China, hundreds of miles away from the capital, Lhassa—a wild, scantily-peopled waste of steppe.

The advocates of the line *viâ* Simla admit to a certain extent the truth of these objections; that is to say, they admit the simple geographical facts, but they deny the conclusions drawn from them; they deny that a more direct communication with Lhassa would prove of advantage to trade.

The staples of our commerce with Chinese Tartary are wool and borax; and these articles come, *not* from the vicinity of the capital, Lhassa, but from districts hundreds of miles away to the north-west, from the wool-producing countries of Gartok and Rudok, and the salt lakes of Ladak—from the wild, scantily-peopled waste of steppe, in fact, which a road *debouching* at Shipkee would connect with Hindostan, not with Bengal Proper only, as would be the case with a line of road *viâ* Darjeeling, but with the populous provinces and busy cities of the north-west—with Umritsur, the Manchester of the Punjab—with Bombay, *viâ* the Indus and Kurrachee—and with England, *viâ* Bombay.

And when to these arguments in favour of the Kalka and Shipkee route, is added the fact, that of its total length of 270 miles the whole has been surveyed, and 177 miles of good road actually constructed, and that roads *viâ* Mussouri and Darjeeling have not been even commenced,* its most strenuous opposers must at least admit that it is worth while to continue the road to Shipkee, and so to test by actual experience the truth or fallacy of the views of its supporters—the utility or uselessness of the scheme.

A reference to the map will show that the wool of

* The elevation of the mountain ridges over which a road *viâ* Mussouri or Darjeeling would have to cross, is so great that it is to be doubted whether such a line could ever be made available for traffic. It would probably be only open for *a few days* in the year, whereas the Simla road never would reach a greater height than 14,000 feet, and would be open for *four months* certain every year.—Author.

Rudok and Gartok can be brought to Shipkee without entering the territories of the Rajah of Kashmir; this fact alone is sufficient to insure its reaching Shipkee, even if greater obstacles to its transit existed; for indemnity from the enormous way-dues exacted by the Kashmir government would amply compensate for the drawback of a slightly longer journey: indeed, it is more than probable that a large portion of the wool of Yarkund would find its way to Shipkee.

The establishment of large fairs along the line of the New Road would greatly encourage trade — thither would flock in crowds the shawl-merchants of Noorpoor, Loodiana, and Umritsur, for then they could purchase in larger quantities and at a much smaller outlay than at present, that precious "*pushm*" which now reaches them in a scanty stream, and with a value doubled by the imposts consequent on its enforced transit through Ladak. The fair at Rampoor, the capital of Bussahir, situate close to the line of the Hindostan and Thibet road, is even now a busy scene, despite the obstacles of mountain passes and unbridged rivers; and from this the conclusion may be safely drawn that the attendance at fairs established at different points along a level road in the same vicinity would be augmented proportionably as the facilities of communication were increased. Nor is this somewhat sanguine view of things Utopian—it is simply the natural result of a good road, as has been proved by experience all over the world.

A happier state of things as far as regards our political position with reference to China, is of course essential to the success of the Hindostan and Thibet road in a commercial point of view; and the restrictions laid on traffic with us by that power must be removed; but it is not until we have opened out a practicable means of communication across the Himalayas that we shall be in a position to demand a concession which, without such means of communication, would be comparatively useless.

At present it would seem that we have sown and others have reaped—we have sown with a lavish hand the seeds of blood and treasure, and the Russians have gathered into their garners the ripe harvest of amicable intercourse and peaceful interchange of commerce which we have failed to realize!

THE END.